P9-CQI-543

LETTERS TO BERNADETTE

The Roy and Landry Families – an Abbreviated Genealogy

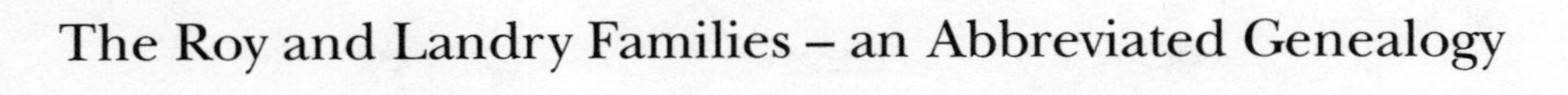

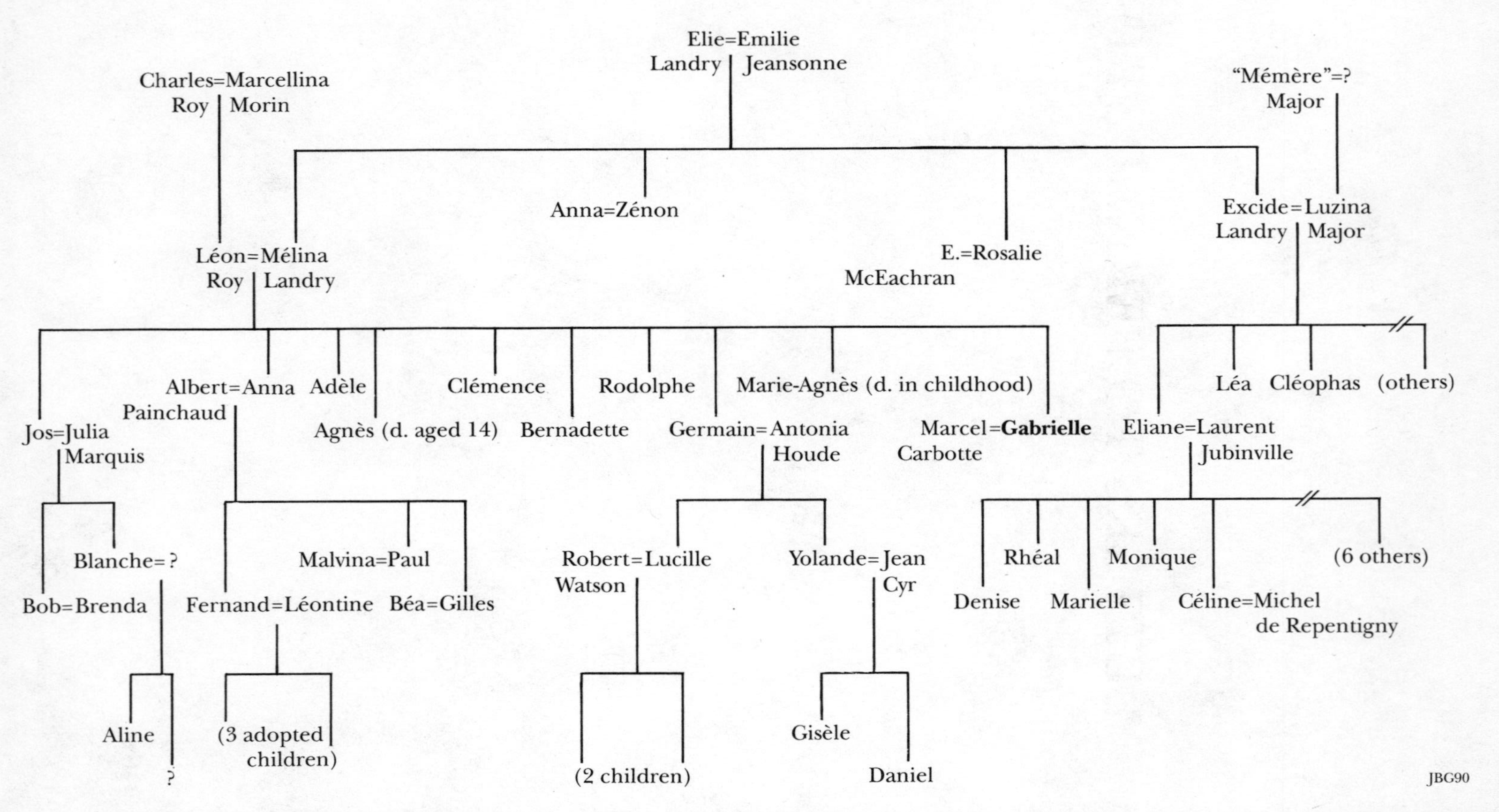

Letters to Bernadette

Gabrielle Roy

Translated by Patricia Claxton

With an introduction by François Ricard

Originally published in French under the title *Ma Chère Petite Soeur,* by Les Editions du Boréal Express, copyright © Fonds Gabrielle Roy, 1988

FIRST EDITION

Canadian Cataloguing in Publication Data

Roy, Gabrielle, 1909-1983
Letters to Bernadette

1st ed.
Translation of: Ma chère petite soeur.
ISBN 0-88619-247-1 (bound) ISBN 0-88619-265-X (pbk.)

1. Roy, Gabrielle, 1909-1983 - Correspondence.
2. Roy, Bernadette, 1897-1970 - Correspondence.
3. Novelists, Canadian (French) - 20th century - Correspondence.* I. Title.

PS8535.0826Z54613 1990 C843'.54 C90-093070-5
PQ3919.R742Z48513 1990

The Publisher wishes to acknowledge the support of the Canada Council and the Ontario Arts Council.

Design by Gordon Robertson
Printed and bound in Canada by
T. H. Best Printing Company Limited

Lester & Orpen Dennys Limited
78 Sullivan Street
Toronto, Canada M5T 1C1

Front photo: Gabrielle Roy in 1943, photo Larose
Back photo: Gabrielle at eighteen months, with Bernadette

Contents

Translator's Note

Gabrielle Roy's letters to Bernadette have a freshness and spontaneity of a kind that finds its way into books perhaps only through personal correspondence. Although there is certainly more forethought to the letters after Bernadette falls seriously ill, the spontaneity does not really disappear; what is new is a depth and intensity of emotion that are glimpsed but not sustained in the family chit-chat and ups and down of events and preoccupations in the previous letters. Yet it is through the earlier exchanges that the affection between the sisters has grown and deepened. I have been very conscious of these things in my translation, as well as of the fact that spontaneity and polish, while not mutually exclusive, are found in different proportions in personal letters as compared to writing intended for publication.

The phrase *Ma chère petite soeur,* with which Gabrielle Roy opens most of these letters, has a special significance. Bernadette's religious name was Soeur Léon de la Croix, or Soeur Léon for short, and it was by this that her order required her to call herself and be called by others. When Gabrielle addressed her as *ma chère petite soeur* she was using the word *soeur* in the double sense of "sister", and avoiding the formal name, which she found forbidding. François Ricard explains this in a note fairly late in the book. Being aware of it at the outset may be helpful to English readers.

The special significance of this phrase was the principal reason for leaving the letter openings in French. It was important to keep the double meaning, yet it seemed odd in English to address someone twelve years older as one's "little sister", since we equate "big" and "little" with size or relative age. During childhood, when sheer size leaves no doubt, the French words *grand* and *petit* relate as naturally as "big" and "little" to both size and age; in later life, *grand* still relates to size but *petit* often simply indicates affection. So does *enfant,* interestingly enough; an affectionately regarded adult (who may be bigger, older, or both) is quite readily called *mon enfant.* Thus, in the later letters, we find the words "My child, my sister" as recurring allusions to Baudelaire's landmark poem, *L'invitation au voyage.* The letter openings in French, where they vary from the key phrase, are not difficult to fathom. Elsewhere, I trust the reader will not be misled by such seeming aberrations as "dear little sister" and "dear child".

Since the French closings are often very foreign to English, I have adapted these, lest they bewilder the reader and intrude on the substance and tone of the letters.

As for certain minor illogicalities and inconsistencies, those attributable to Gabrielle Roy's personal interpretation remain intact, but occasionally, where her mind has been quicker than her hand, I have made slight adjustments so that anomalies will not distract the reader from more important things. For instance, after the birthday party for Gabrielle organized by Bernadette in her hospital room, Gabrielle recalls details of the scene, where all was pervaded by "the vital presence of your love bringing life to everything around, penetrating the walls of your hospital room to find and envelop me with warmth"; yet Gabrielle was *in* the room during the party; she must also have been thinking of the hours following the party after she had left Bernadette's room, and so I felt compelled to add the phrase "wherever I was". There is no such intervention where, for example, Gabrielle speaks of the evening mass at Saint Dominique Church as beginning variously at five o'clock, a quarter to five, or a quarter past five, although the actual time must surely have been consistent.

I have not corrected small errors in quotations from English poets for the similar reason that Gabrielle Roy is quoting from memory. Except for three lines which she quotes in English, the English versions of all quotations are mine.

Gabrielle Roy's paragraphing, which is not always strictly logical, remains as in the French. Pronouns relating to God are in lower case, following her own customary though not consistent practice and reflecting her very personal relationship to God. Postscripts in italics indicate afterthoughts squeezed into margins or whatever other space was available on a page already full.

As a result of François Ricard's continuing research since the publication of the original French edition of this book, an undated postcard has been repositioned and some small details in the notes have been changed. I have added a few notes and slightly modified several others to provide information of interest to English readers. I have also drawn up an abbreviated genealogical table which is far from complete but which, I hope, will help readers to situate family members mentioned by name or relationship here and in *Enchantment and Sorrow*, Gabrielle Roy's autobiography. At this point it has not been firmly established where Gabrielle Roy's cousin Eva fits into this table.

I would like to express my thanks to François Ricard, who has been unfailingly understanding and helpful in shedding light on many aspects of Gabrielle Roy's life and work, and to Gena Gorrell, whose editorial guidance has been invaluable. I would also like to thank Yolande Roy-Cyr, Joan Rolland, Sister Pauline Martin, Jori Smith, and the Service de la faune, Ministère du loisir, de la chasse et de la pêche du Québec, whom I have consulted on various points and who have been most generous with their time and interest.

Patricia Claxton

Introduction

Bernadette Roy was born on September 15, 1897, and was therefore twelve years older than Gabrielle. Although she was the youngest of the first four Roy sisters[1], she and Gabrielle had little opportunity to know each other in their youth, for Bernadette left home at an early age. After working for a time as a lay teacher, she entered religious life in 1919, joining the sisters of Les Saints Noms de Jésus et Marie (The Holy Names of Jesus and Mary), and left Saint-Boniface to begin her novitiate in Montreal[2]. She returned in 1921 after taking her vows and assuming the name of Sister Léon-de-la-Croix. Then began her long career as a teaching nun, including twenty years "on mission" in Kenora and Keewatin, at the extreme western edge of Ontario. When Bernadette finally came back to settle in Saint-Boniface, where she taught at the Académie Saint-Joseph until her retirement in 1966, Gabrielle had already left Manitoba and was living in Quebec City.

Although the two sisters were separated for most of their lives, they were always very close. They were drawn to each other initially by a kind of mutual understanding arising from shared sensitivities and their warmth, enthusiasm, and inquiring minds, qualities in sharp contrast to the rather dour atmosphere prevalent in the family circle. In *Enchantment and Sorrow*, the autobiography Gabrielle Roy wrote in the last years of her life, the author nostalgically recalls Sister Léon's visits to the house on Deschambault Street and the pleasure these visits brought for them both[3]. She recalls as well that when the time came for her to leave Manitoba and try her luck in Europe, Bernadette was the only one of the family, almost the only person she knew, who understood and encouraged her to go[4].

Gabrielle and Bernadette stayed in touch subsequently through a continued exchange of letters, which not only kept them from drifting apart with advancing age but actually brought them closer together, as each came to appreciate and cherish the other even more than before. Every summer, from her community's summer camp on the shores of

Lake Winnipeg, Bernadette wrote long, ecstatic letters for Gabrielle, extolling the beauties of the world and the joy of existence. Gabrielle replied, writing of her own joys and also of her troubles. And Bernadette always consoled or reassured her. Although only Gabrielle's letters are assembled in this volume, among their most striking revelations is the deep, firm friendship between the two sisters, their confidence in one another, their uncomplicated, unalloyed tenderness and compassion for one another, all increasing as the years pass and experiences and shared bereavements accumulate. It was only natural in the end for the younger sister to help the older to die.

In *Enchantment and Sorrow*, Gabrielle Roy speaks a number of times of Bernadette's death on May 25, 1970, and of the weeks that preceded it. In March, as soon as she learned that Bernadette was very seriously ill with cancer of the kidney, she left Quebec City for Saint-Boniface, where she stayed for three weeks, visiting her sister every day and trying to bring her comfort. Then:

> After I left, during the weeks she had remaining, I wrote her a letter every day, sometimes twice a day, always trying to persuade her that she'd felt the splendours of life more vibrantly than anyone else. [. . .] Dédette and I, who'd never had much chance to get to know each other, became so close we began to feel inseparable[5].

* * *

In this book are assembled 138 previously unpublished letters written by Gabrielle Roy to Bernadette. They begin in 1943, when Gabrielle, who had returned from Europe four years earlier, was a journalist in Montreal and was writing *The Tin Flute.* They cease in 1970 with Bernadette's death.

This correspondence divides unmistakably into two major parts, each with its own special if not exclusive interest. The first part extends from the earliest of the letters to that of March 6, 1970 — in other words, from the year in which their mother died until Gabrielle learned that her favourite sister was soon to die. The letters of this period of almost three decades are somewhat spasmodic and their content is more or less anecdotal. Yet they are unquestionably of biographical interest, containing valuable information about the life, thinking, and personality of Gabrielle Roy, the origins of some of her writings, the evolution of her writer's powers of observation and reflection, her private worries, and so on. In particular, they show the importance Gabrielle Roy attached to her relations with her family, confirming — or documenting, which is more to the point, perhaps — one of the essential themes in *Enchantment and Sorrow*.

The second part comprises the letters written in March, April, and May 1970, in the weeks immediately preceding the death of Bernadette. These letters speak of death, but they also speak eloquently of love, and out of the anguish that attended their writing grew, paradoxically, the sense of oneness with the universe expressed by Gabrielle Roy in *Enchanted Summer*[6]. Although they were not written for publication, I believe they rank with the best of her writing. They illustrate superbly her deft way of imparting feeling, her gift for emotional resonance — what I would call the compassion in writing that so strongly imprints and distinguishes Gabrielle Roy's works. The literary value of these letters is thus beyond question.

* * *

Before being consigned to the National Library of Canada in 1984, these letters were kept by Gabrielle Roy herself, to whom they had been given on the death of her sister[7]. With them were found only four or five written by Bernadette, which are not reproduced here.

The handwritten correspondence was faithfully reproduced in the French edition of this book, *Ma chère petite soeur: Lettres à Bernadette, 1943-1970*, published in 1988. My editorial interventions were limited to correcting some spelling and grammatical errors, adding dates to a few letters, omitting a few personal names[8], dividing the letters into several chapters reflecting my perception of the pace and thematic development of the correspondence, and, most of all, adding notes and clarifications where this appeared necessary for full understanding of the text[9].

In conclusion, I wish to thank those whose help I received in the preparation of this correspondence for publication: the late Doctor Marcel Carbotte of Quebec City, who enlightened me on a number of details; Claude Le Moine and Irma Larouche of the National Library of Canada, custodians of the Gabrielle Roy papers; Lise Faubert of McGill University, who transcribed the manuscripts; and the Killam Fellowship Program of the Canada Council, whose assistance enabled much earlier publication of the book than would otherwise have been possible.

François Ricard
Executive Director
Fonds Gabrielle Roy

Notes to Introduction

1. Gabrielle Roy, the youngest of the family, had four sisters and three brothers. In descending order of seniority, they were Jos, Anna, Adèle, Clémence, Bernadette, Rodolphe, and Germain. Two other sisters, also born before Gabrielle, died in childhood.
2. Bernadette's entry into religious life inspired a story in *Street of Riches*, "A Bit of Yellow Ribbon".
3. See *Enchantment and Sorrow*, p. 102-104.
4. See *Enchantment and Sorrow* p. 169-171.
5. See *Enchantment and Sorrow* p. 126-127, 172.
6. See *Enchantment and Sorrow* p. 172-173.
7. These 138 letters are probably not the only ones Gabrielle Roy wrote to Bernadette; some written before 1943 are certainly missing, and perhaps some written later. But there cannot be many.
8. These names, which are indeed few, have been omitted either out of respect for the privacy of certain living persons or at the express wish of Gabrielle Roy. Textual omissions of this nature are indicated by square brackets. The names of living family members are intact, following Gabrielle Roy's own practice in *Enchantment and Sorrow*.
9. These notes and clarifications, indicated by number in the text, will be found at the back of the book.

LETTERS TO BERNADETTE

1943 — 1947

Ford Hotel, Montreal, September 15, 1943

Chère soeur Bernadette,

This is the first time I've written you since the day we stood arm and arm, you and I, gazing at the little body that had been our mother[1]. My dear, kind sister, that day as never before I felt the strength in you, God's great serenity in you. And if I haven't written you since, it's not because I haven't thought about this every single day: you and I beside that little body — all we loved most in the world. Dear, dear Dédette, my big sister of my childhood — at a moment when I was feeling so alone, so bereft that life no longer seemed to have any purpose or direction, this was still what you were to me, my big sister. Thank you for the comfort you gave me.

As you know, I spent the summer in the Gaspé[2]. For now I'm back in Montreal, where I couldn't find anywhere to lay my head except a hotel because we're in the midst of a housing crisis here, besides having all the headaches of the high cost of living, etc., etc. The war is making itself felt increasingly on this overpopulated city, which has become almost hysterical. Really, people are crazy, you know, crazy with sorrow, bewilderment, guilt, and anxiety. Where in all of this is there anything to remind us of Christ's teachings about loving one another?

Anyway, what I'm really trying to say is that I'm only here until I leave again to research some articles.

For the time being, please write me care of the *Bulletin des agriculteurs*[3].

Are you back at your teaching? How are you? Poor you, the shocks of the summer must have put a strain on your health. As for me, my stay in the Gaspé was fairly good for me. I was boarding with some humble folk who were warm and unpretentious, which always puts me at ease and relaxes my nerves. I really don't think I'll ever like city life. The country with its straightforward, hardworking people, slow pace of living, and wide-open horizons, all this I really do think I love with the same passion dear Maman had for the country. Like her, every spring I feel the need to breathe the smell of freshly turned earth and find myself on a country highway, travelling contentedly towards the horizon. You'll see how well Anna[4] describes the lure that the country had for Maman in the letter she asked me to send on to you.

I haven't forgotten Clémence[5], you know. I believe Maman left her to us as a guarantee of salvation, of redemption; that she left her to us so we'd know that it's good to make sacrifices. I try to write to her often, and I help her live decently. And that at least is a great comfort to me.

Dear Dédette, from the depth of my loneliness — a loneliness that calls aloud and won't be still since Maman died — I send you my love and a big hug like the ones I used to give you when I was little and you were my big sister.

Gabrielle

Rawdon[6], January 4 [1946]

Ma chère soeur,
I intended to write you for Christmas, you know, but I simply didn't have time just then. Anyway, I hope you understood and knew I was thinking of you most lovingly on Christmas Day, and tenderly reminiscing, imagining you all — you, Clémence, Adèle[7], and Anna, together again with our dear Maman in the house on Deschambault Street[8]. This is where my thoughts always turn at Christmastime.

I'm so glad you were able to see Anna and even spend an afternoon with her. You have stayed so natural, so vivacious, that I can imagine your joy, beautiful like a child's in the exuberant way you show it. Anna too told me about it, and I was delighted and sad both at once . . . sad not to be there with you.

You wrote me a most charming letter which really touched me. Your dear little calendar with Jesus in blue is already pinned up on the wall of my room, and it keeps reminding me how good you are to me.

I did indeed also receive the nicest possible letter from Sister Diomède. It will be a great pleasure to write her in reply because I always liked her, and besides, during my convent years I think she showed me more about what is beautiful than any other teacher, and helped me choose my career by giving me the encouragement I needed.

I'll drop a line to Sister Albert-de-Jésus as well. I've had so much to do in the past few months, you know, I'm way behind in my correspondence.

My book is really a great success and I'm more surprised than anyone else. Did Anna tell you I'd signed a contract with a big New York publisher, who will publish a translation of my book? It will probably come out in the United States some time next autumn[9]. That could mean a lot of money, and as you can imagine, being well off will make me happy for a number of reasons, especially for protecting Clémence against whatever might befall her.

After three months in Montreal I was glad to get back to Rawdon, where at least I can work in peace and solitude, two conditions that I absolutely must have.

For entertainment, since life here is very quiet — sometimes even too quiet — I read a lot in the evenings, and believe it or not, I also amuse myself making patchwork quilts like the ones Grand'mère used to make. My elderly landlady taught me how, and I think I've made something really quite different and even pretty.

For the moment, my trip to the West is postponed. What is not so pleasant about the life of a writer is having to attend to all kinds of business matters . . . and mine were pretty chaotic. So I've had to stay put to look after my affairs. I haven't given up my plan to come West, and I look forward to dropping in and giving you a hug when I do come. But I don't want you to be disappointed so don't expect me soon . . . and if it's a surprise when I turn up, so much the better, don't you think?

The photograph of me that you like so much was taken last

autumn, say a little more than a year ago. It's very good, I agree, but most of the credit goes to Madame Zarov, one of the finest portrait photographers in Canada[10]. If you'd been in Montreal recently you would have been really amazed to see me (in pictures of course) on display in the big bookstores, in Eaton's and other places. I found it all pretty hard to bear, but publicity, it seems, is very necessary. And then, the public is insisting more and more on knowing the author of a book. At least here in Rawdon my private life is my own, and I like it that way.

For the good people of this big village, I haven't changed; I'm still "the little girl who boards at Mother Tinkler's". It brings me back to a proper sense of values, or would if I were tempted to think myself too grand.

But you know, Dédette, all this to-do over my name hasn't changed me or gone to my head at all. Of course, I'm pleased if you, Adèle, and Anna feel proud of me in a way. I wish most of all that Maman were still alive to share in the family satisfaction; yes, that would be marvellous.

Well, I wasn't paying attention and my letter has grown very long. How are you? You don't ever really tell me in your letters.

Your prayers for me touch my heart and unquestionably help me. Thank you and please keep offering God your great honesty and piety for me.

And may you always have this tranquil joy of a soul at peace that you've possessed so long, and that you spread to everyone around you.

Affectionately,

Gabrielle

Saint-Vital[11], May 10, 1947

Ma chère soeur,

Many thanks for your letter. As you've realized, I thought it best to come straight to Winnipeg without stopping in Kenora[12], mostly because I was worried about Anna and Clémence. Anna is much better.

She has been home for two days and I think she's still reasonably well. She certainly has extraordinary reserves of strength and energy. As for Clémence, I found her so weak I put her in hospital for a series of tests. So far the tests and X-rays have shown nothing serious, but she'll stay in hospital another week for more tests and some medication. I'm also trying to find her a boarding house, because we can't leave her in a room by herself any longer or she'll eat like a bird. You know how hard it is to get her to do anything. She doesn't care much about living, so she has become very resistant to any help or advice. I do have some influence with her but I confess I'm awfully worried and discouraged about what may become of her. I had hoped to be able to take her back with me, but I can't look after her as constantly as she needs. I don't have any fixed address yet, or anything I can call home. So for the moment I think it would be wiser to put her either with an understanding family or in an institution. As you can see, these worries are taking up all my time; I'm not used to this kind of thing and for the moment can't think about anything else. When I've decided what to do about the most immediate problem I'll let you know. What Clémence needs most is a place where she'll be guided, advised, treated with kindness, and still have little things to do to make her feel useful, without which life becomes unbearable. So pray that I'll unearth such a place, because Clémence's lot is my biggest concern. I can't make any other plans at the moment because I came quickly, as soon as I heard that Anna was in hospital again.

I had the pleasure of seeing Sister Diomède and several other nuns from the Académie. You can read how I dropped in unexectedly to see them in a fairly accurate account in *La Liberté*[13].

I haven't much time now to write everything I'd like to tell you. I hope to do so soon.

Meanwhile, my fondest love,

Gabrielle

Saint-Vital, May 19, 1947

Ma chère enfant,

I'm writing with the beautiful pen you gave me, a treasured reminder of your visit. We miss you and are sorry you had to leave. It was so good for us all to have you here. Perhaps for me more than anyone else; your devotion and love for us warmed my heart immensely. And that was what I needed most.

Before I'm able to thank Sister Albert-de-Jésus myself for her thoughtfulness in sending you to see us, would you do me a favour and give her a message for me? Tell her I very much appreciate her generosity and kind consideration.

I'm also going to ask you to get as much rest as possible, for in this sad, difficult world, little saints like you come bearing a light that is most necessary. I'd be so pleased if you could manage to spare your strength, slow down and put less energy into the job you're doing. Won't you try, just to please me?

I'll write later and send you word about Clémence. She's very cheerful this morning and full of chatter, telling us every last detail about her stay in hospital. She has her own little adventure to tell now, which boosts her self-esteem and makes her feel interesting.

Much love to you,

Gabrielle

1948 — 1950

Paris[14], January 22, 1948

Ma chère petite soeur,
It's been such a long time since I had the pleasure of walking up Quality Hill nearly every evening, entering the convent and at once finding myself bathed in peace and tranquillity. These lovely memories are far away indeed, here in Paris — where, more than anywhere else, the social instability of a world in disorder is apparent to an extreme degree. But we haven't suffered much, Marcel and I, except in little ways, for which we're none the worse. Paris is still an exciting and captivating city. The men who built this city had a sense of beauty you'll search in vain for among the builders of today. Three weeks' holiday in Switzerland have done us a great deal of good, however, because life is simpler there than in France and the people, having been spared the war, radiate an aura of calm and common sense. And food is plentiful besides. In short, we had a happy time in this wonderfully orderly little country; its tidiness makes up for a good many human follies [elsewhere]!

Marcel sends you his best regards. He thinks of you often. He's very fond of you and admires you too. Your prayers must have worked well for me, because I couldn't hope for a better life companion than Marcel. He is most unusually thoughtful and sensitive.

I hope your health is better, and so does Marcel. Do you like being at Saint-Jean-Baptiste[15]? You must miss your lovely Lake of the Woods. I'd like to hear that you're not overdoing things. I know you, a bit of a whirlwind, always wound up, throwing yourself into the hardest part of any task without a thought for your own weakened condition. You must be sensible and try to do only what you're able to. I really worry about you, you know, and hope you don't have too heavy a work load and do have a good doctor. You must be sure to go and see him, too, and let him take care of you. No doctor can work miracles and cure people who don't do anything to help themselves.

In December I sent you a cheque for $1,000 as a donation for educational works. I'd like you to send me a receipt, dated 1947 if possible, so I can put it on my income tax return for this year. This way, I may be able to make another donation for 1948.

The news I'm getting from Anna about Clémence is not reassuring. The poor soul has fallen into a deplorable state of slovenliness again. I don't know what to do. I've tried everything. We'll just have to hope. I'd be grateful if you would write to her and try to cheer her up a bit.

Dear little sister, it's a bit late but I wish you a year of peace and happiness. Better health, too, and the joy you've always had, which to my mind comes of a pure and generous heart.

My fondest love,

Gabrielle

Paris, June 22, 1948

Ma chère petite soeur,
It's good to sit down and write to you for a few minutes. Your last letter brought much delight to both of us. I think I've already answered it, but never mind, I enjoy saying again that your letters bring us sweet memories of happy times at Kenora.

I have written to Lucille[16] and will help her with her studies. Later on it will be her turn to help her younger sister, and this way, I hope, a little good will end up bringing much happiness. I hope also to send you some money that you can share equally with Clémence, if you will. This way she'll have a little something put by to ensure her some peace of mind in case I'm not able to keep on helping her later. She's in such a state that we have to make sure she's provided for. I would like Adèle to have some money too, but she told me she didn't want to accept anything of the sort. Sister dear, when you go to Saint-Boniface I would appreciate your asking Clémence if she has a chequebook and if she knows how to get money from the bank in case she needs it. She's so bad about replying when I ask her questions that I haven't yet been able to find out. So it's a point I'm counting on you to clear up for me. It won't do any good to put money in her bank account if she won't even learn to write cheques when necessary. I don't think I'll be able to send you this money until the autumn, but it will be this year, in any event.

Through a Canadian[17] friend who is going back to Canada this summer, I'm sending you a little present consisting of some pictures and a poem by Péguy illustrated with some views of Chartres. Through this same friend I'm also sending some other little presents which I'd be grateful if you would distribute; a book for Yolande[18], a silk handkerchief and a little bottle of perfume for Anna, a collar and other small things for Clémence. You may not get them until late summer. I thought it best to have them all sent to you because I couldn't ask this friend to make three parcels. I hope it won't be a bother for you to distribute them.

The weather has been awful for weeks on end. Rain almost every day. I'm waiting for the warmth and sunshine and then will go and spend several weeks by the sea. I want very much to see something of Brittany, and anyway, to be honest, around this time of year I begin to detest cities and long to be in the country.

Did you start a little garden this year? Do you still believe so strongly in the benefits of carrots? They're a vegetable we rarely see in Paris restaurants, though I don't know why. I've started another collection of postcards for you, which I'll send soon.

I hope your health really has improved and you're not just saying so. Do try to rest this summer and not take on anything beyond your strength.

A big hug from each of us and much, much love.

Gabrielle

Saint-Germain-en-Laye[19], October 18, 1948

Ma chère soeur,

I think my last letter to you must have gone astray because I've received no reply to my many questions about Clémence. However, Marcel received the very kind letter you addressed to him personally. He was touched and delighted by it.

Did you get the little presents I sent by way of Mlle Lapointe[20], a book for you, a scarf and perfume for Anna, etc.?

You'll soon be receiving a cheque from Maître J.-M. Nadeau[21] for a thousand dollars, made out to the Parish of Keewatin[22].

If you can get Adèle to accept some money I would be very pleased. I don't know what Clémence has left in the bank. She never answers my questions about things like that. Her little letters are like the ones I used to write when I was at convent, always about spring arriving or autumn returning — purely philosophical considerations or else vague descriptions. I really believe that if she didn't have a cent left she'd still just keep telling me what the weather was like in Saint-Boniface. She's so much more detached from the details of daily life than the rest of us that I sometimes find myself thinking of her as the one with the loftiest spirit. Anyway, her funny little letters don't let me know much about the conditions she's living in and I'd be grateful if you would do a little investigating on that score. Perhaps Adèle and Clémence could share some money. Do what you think best, and thank you in advance. Also, don't forget to send me a receipt as soon as you can.

We've moved, as you can see. Every time we do, the new place seems infinitely better at first than what we've just left, so I'll wait a while before crying "Success!" Still, there are a lot of advantages where we are now, and the first is that we're living very close to Paris — 21 kilometres, or about 15 miles — in an almost rustic retreat. We can get to Paris on very frequent electric trains. Besides, Saint-Germain is an extremely interesting town, the site of one of the really old châteaux of the kings of France, as you know. Louis XIV lived here — was born here, in fact — then left for Versailles, which was more to his taste for pomp and glory. But most important, this was the home of Good King Henry IV, whom I'll always like because one day he said he wanted "a chicken in every pot on Sundays". The town is surrounded by the huge, tall Forest of Saint-Germain, which at this time of year is a paradise for meditation, with the lovely colouring of its leaves and the sound of berries and chestnuts falling softly through the silence.

My dear little sister, we both send you a big, affectionate hug. Write soon.

Your loving sister,

Gabrielle

Saint-Germain-en-Laye, June 13, 1949

Ma chère petite soeur,
I received your letter just this morning and am replying without delay. I did indeed receive your lovely long New Year's letter and had thought I'd answered it, but perhaps I didn't, and I'm really sorry to have taken so long to write and give you our news.

I've been feeling better in the last two months. Before that I was in rather a bad way, with almost constant pains in my stomach, and terribly tired. I went to see another specialist, who prescribed a treatment very different from the first I was given, and I've been feeling much better since. Anyway, don't worry because I have no cause for complaint now.

Marcel is still working hard, and we haven't yet decided when we'll be returning to Canada. I think it would be advantageous for him to finish up his studies here, which means another six months perhaps. In any event, we're going to take a holiday this year. Marcel needs it because his work at the laboratory is very tiring. Perhaps we'll go to the seaside for a month or two.

I'm glad you were able to go and see Clémence. If Adèle would be willing to move back to Manitoba and look after Clémence, this might well be the best solution. I worry constantly about Clémence, and about Adèle too.

I'll soon be sending you another cheque, probably for $1,000. If you share it with Adèle and Clémence, I think this, added to Clémence's pension, should allow them to live fairly decently.

I wrote to Anna and received a lovely letter in reply. I do so wish I found her better and in a more contented frame of mind. I'm sure your prayers have been a great help to her, as they are to us all. Thank you for thinking so often of me, and with such affection. I'm happy to hear you're feeling stronger. What you need most is rest, more than an hour a day, I should think. Do try to get as much as you can. Are you going to have a holiday this year? You love nature so much, I'm hoping with all my heart that you'll be able to spend some time in the country. I often think of you at the little convent in Kenora, and I can still see you sitting on the porch with the evening light you found so beautiful descending on the lake. You felt the grace of nature so intensely that very often I too was moved by it, through you. Here, I have the magnificent Forest of Saint-Germain close by and often go for walks there in the afternoon. In just a few minutes I can be on paths that are totally peaceful, and what a joy it is then to feel myself enfolded in the shade and greenery of those enormous trees. Sometimes I go for a second walk in the evening with Marcel. Once we were so entranced with the path we were following that we let ourselves be drawn along it much farther than we should have. When we came to the edge of the forest just at nightfall, the countryside was deep blue, an atmosphere so inviting that we kept walking towards the nearest villages. I could hardly drag one foot behind the other on the way home. I didn't mind, because nothing satisfies me as much as a long walk, especially at twilight, the hour of in-between. In Manitoba too, this was the time I always liked best, and at Uncle Excide's[23] when I was a child I remember yearning for twilight to come, I so loved to emerge from the woods at that hour and set off up the lovely road leading towards Saint-Léon[24].

You tell me that Sister Marie-de-l'Assomption is fond of me. I'm particularly touched to hear this because I've always thought she was an exceptional woman in both intellect and sensitivity. Do give her my thanks for continuing to remember me so faithfully.

I'm back to work again a bit and what I've done is perhaps quite good. I'm a poor judge of my own work. I've been writing mostly articles and short stories, some of them inspired by scenes of life in France that I've gathered during our few trips. The rest, on the other hand, have been dictated by homesickness[25]. Oddly, people and places that I might not have thought very interesting when I was at home seem positively fascinating now that I'm here. Distance stirs curious feelings inside us. It awakens affection for many things we never knew we loved. From here, I can see how incomparably beautiful, youthful, and dynamic life is in Canada. It's different here: you live amid elegance of form, colour, works of art, and you have to partake of all this refinement in order to appreciate things that are less polished but have another kind of beauty. How many splendid churches there are in France! Even the most inconsequential village has one that puts our most sumptuous cathedrals to shame. What a delight nature is in France! Particularly in Ile-de-France. Everywhere you turn you see forests, winding rivers, and marvellous orchards of peach, pear, cherry, and apple trees. Everything is so tidy that even when you look at a vegetable garden you can recognize the overriding French love of balance, logic, and moderation. We have made friends with some very fine people and I can't tell you how much we're enriched by their company. It's such a pleasure to hear a cultivated, elegant French spoken naturally and without affectation. We see the Béclères (Doctor Béclère is a distinguished French gynecologist), the Moricards (another family of doctors), sometimes the Vaniers (the Canadian ambassador)[26]. I don't go out much, though, because nothing tires me more than social events. We rarely accept invitations, and only when the hosts are people who genuinely like us.

You may know that Paula Sumner[27] is in France with her children, her husband, and even her mother. They're all living in a suburb of Paris not far from us and we've seen them two or three times already. We took them to Chartres one Sunday. It was my third time there and I was still discovering this marvel among cathedrals. The stained-glass windows had all been put back in place by then[28]. It was marvellous. Paula was delighted with the trip. Mother Sumner too. I think they're going to be in France for a year, so we'll have the pleasure of seeing some more of each other.

Marcel sends you his brotherly greetings. Do give us another letter before too long.

Affectionately,

Gabrielle

Saint Germain-en-Laye, October 24, 1949

Ma chère petite soeur,
How I enjoyed your lovely kind letter! Thank you so much; I'm hoping I'll soon have another that's just as full of news. I was distressed, however, to hear of Sister Maxima's death. She was always very good to me; her memory is inseparable from my last year of convent, and from English poetry; she appreciated it so keenly and was so good at awakening that appreciation in others. In particular, as I recall, her love of beauty turned her instinctively towards Keats, one of the purest of English poets, and she used to read him with a warmth and affection that brought out his wistfulness and musicality. Poor little Sister Maxima — she used to read "A thing of beauty is a joy for ever" so lovingly.

I've sent you a cheque for a thousand dollars through Maître Jean-Marie Nadeau[29]. Would you be kind enough to send me a receipt as soon as you get it. Would you send the usual portions to our two sisters who are so much in need, and join me in thanking God for allowing me to provide them with this material help.

Affectionately,

Gabrielle

Saint-Germain-en-Laye, May 11, 1950

Ma chère soeur,
I've just read your dear little letter with great joy. Of all the letters I get from Canada, yours bring me the most pleasure. We've been thinking of you these last few days, Marcel and I, because even in *Le Figaro* they've been talking daily about the floods in Winnipeg. I can't tell you how worried we are about Anna, Fernand[30], everybody in fact, because the papers here don't give any details and we're inclined to imagine the worst. I hope we'll soon have word that no one in the family has had too hard a time of it. Anna's the one we're most worried about, she's so near the river.

I'm delighted to hear your news. You'll benefit marvellously from the diction lessons you're planning to take this summer, I'm sure. I'm glad to be helping you carry through with something you really want to do. I hope you won't work too hard, though. It's very hot in Montreal in summer. I'm afraid you may find it very tiring there. And then all these things, lessons to take here, your teaching there, are leaving you without any real holiday, and you really need one. I don't want to throw cold water on your enthusiasm, far from it, and I admire you for undertaking things you could perfectly well leave to others, but still, I wonder if you aren't taxing your energy and health unreasonably. I know something of this because I'm now coping with the same disorder you've had. I too have a small goitre and all the signs of hyperthyroidism [*sic*]. Most of all, I'm almost continually tired. They're still reluctant to operate, I don't know why — if it were my decision I'd have the operation right away.

Yes, we will be home this year, perhaps in August but perhaps not until September. We can't settle the date yet. It would be such a shame not to be able to see each other in Montreal. If that's the case we must try to meet somewhere else, and as soon as we can. I can see there are plenty of rumours about us these days in Saint-Boniface. Marcel has not accepted any teaching chair in Quebec. For the moment, although nothing's definite yet, we'll more likely settle in Montreal[31].

Marcel is well and sends you kind and affectionate regards. He's very fond of you. He often says, "Our little sister Dédette has a beautiful soul." I like hearing him say such things about you.

My fondest love,

Gabrielle

1955 — 1960

Port Navalo, June 4, 1955

Chère petite Soeur Léon-de-la-Croix,
When you get this letter you'll probably be very surprised to see that I'm in France — but perhaps you've heard already. Marcel sent me your letter and I received it in Paris. I was there for three weeks and am now taking a rest in the small village of Morbihan, by the sea. I have all the things I love here: a little fishing village, very old and very picturesque; prairies covered with yellow-flowered broom, whose brightness seems to be throwing light towards the rather grey sky. I'm enchanted with the colours, and most of all the ever-present sound of the sea.

I'm so happy for you that you can come to Quebec City[32]. Sad, however, that I won't be there to make you at home. I'm sure Marcel will do it for me, and he'll take you to see some of the sights, to the extent that he's free. I'm sending you a cheque for Clémence's room and board and also $10.00 for you and $10.00 for Adèle.

I made a very quick decision on this trip to France, in fact just ten days before leaving. Which is why I didn't have time to tell anyone in Manitoba. Perhaps I'll be back while you're still in Quebec, but I doubt it because the passage to France is rather expensive and to make it worth while I have to stay several months.

I'm feeling pretty well. The truth is that travelling agrees with me. I'm going to write to Anna, Clémence, and Adèle, but in the meantime will you give them my regards and tell them I think of them often? Don't overtire yourself, especially in these busy, exhausting final days of the school year.

A big, warm hug to you, and I hope you have a lovely, rewarding, and restful summer.

Gabrielle

Since I may not stay here very long, write to Marcel when this cheque arrives and send him a receipt (in duplicate, please). He'll keep it for me.

Quebec City, October 2, 1957

Ma chère petite soeur,

Your delightful little letter arrived just moments ago and I've enjoyed it so much that I'm replying without delay. The thing I love about your short, happy letters is that, although you must often be tired like everyone else, they're always full of life and hope and so they always give me the greatest pleasure. Like you, I hope we'll see poor Clémence go back to the Sisters of the Presentation[33], now that she's learned at last — the hard way, poor thing — that she was better off there than anywhere else. I hope it will happen soon. Yes, I spent the summer in our little cottage in Petite-Rivière-Saint-François[34], where I really believe the view is one of the most beautiful in the world. From the top of a small cliff we overlook the river where it's very wide; on one side there's a line of lovely hills, and below us lies Ile-aux-Coudres, about midway between the two shores. Behind, we have a high mountain covered with maples and birches almost to its peak. A marvellous sight! Unfortunately the sea air, which made me feel well for so many years, now rather tires me, making me short of breath and giving me palpitations. So I've come back to the city rather tired and having lost weight during my holiday, which for me is surprising. Although I enjoyed it — this is the first time in my life that I've ever had my own home — as holidays go it has been tiring because I've been doing a great deal: weeding, looking after the lawn and flowers, and then I've probably been walking too much. However, I've already begun to return to my normal weight and I'm sleeping better. The nights were much too short there. If I can overcome some persisting fatigue I'm going to try to come west. For the moment, since I still so badly need rest, I'm afraid it won't be possible. So pray that I'll regain some energy soon and leave this sluggishness behind. Marcel is very well. His stay [at Petite Rivière] has done him a world of good. Gardening, trotting around all day long in the open air, attending to his little trees, all of this has suited him marvellously and has relaxed him in a way that nothing else does. Seeing him with his flowers sometimes reminds me of our dear old father when he was happily tending his roses and vegetable seedlings, remember? I'd love you to see our little property some day.

I've worked a great deal this summer, but so far I'm not too pleased with what I've done. Perhaps when I take it up again later I'll manage to make something not too bad of it[35].

Continue keeping as close an eye as you can on Clémence. I'm reassured when you do, and relieved of my greatest source of worry. Good luck in your teaching and all your activities, but look after yourself and don't overwork.

Fondest love from us both,

Gabrielle

Quebec City, January 10, 1958

Ma chère petite soeur,
And you in turn have written me a sweet, affectionate letter that touched my heart — if mine really did warm yours, I'm glad. Goodness knows, when you think of it, we survive on these blessed crumbs. I received your calendar, so skilfully made that it reminds me how tirelessly active you are, even finding time for small handicrafts, it seems. All the news in your letter this year is good, generally speaking,

except for Anna's illness, but at least she isn't doing too badly for the moment, perhaps better than during the summer, I gather from what you tell me. I'll be very frank and say that your good news, especially about Clémence, was my best Christmas present this year. You know so well how to soothe my worries about Clémence, about Adèle, about all of you. In your invincible optimism, you find reasons for being happy, for hope, where others would see only gloom. Your optimism has helped me many times, and on balance I think it's the right attitude. Most of all, do keep as close an eye on Clémence as possible to see that she stays in this better condition; it's my greatest comfort for the moment. I think Maman worries less — if it's true that she can still worry — when Clémence shows a little happiness.

I've sent money for several months' room and board in advance, and another bottle of vitamins to Clémence herself, which I do hope she'll keep taking. Incidentally, it occurred to me to write a note of thanks myself to the Sister Superior of the Presentation, and I received a nice reply besides. Everything is fine in that quarter.

Spare your nervous energy, my dear: this is my most urgent advice for the year ahead. I know you're inclined to spend yourself to the last drop of fuel.

Marcel sends his brotherly greetings. I'm enclosing a few lines for Sister Eugène-Amalia.

My fondest love,

Gabrielle

Quebec City, September 3, 1958

Ma chère petite soeur,

Your letter quite enchanted me, a vibrant little letter brimming and bubbling with joy to be back in the midst of nature, which you love so much. I can see you in your rocking chair on a wooden veranda, gazing with delight at the trees and water, your nostrils almost quivering, as always when you're deeply moved. How sweet of you to have shared this moment of joy with me! I do so hope you're rested and fit by now, ready to get down to work again, and that your task will be as undemanding as possible, even easy. I've just received a nice little letter from Clémence, whose health must indeed be better, since she's made the effort to give me some news. Thank goodness for that. It also relieves me to hear that Adèle is going to stay in town and will have that small position at the sanatorium. I wrote to Anna the other day. I'm really afraid that having her two boys visiting will be very tiring for her; both at once is a bit much.

I hope you'll continue to give me news of her from time to time — as far as you can, with everything else you have to do.

Would you thank Sister Malvina[36] very warmly for all the attention she's given Clémence, for all her patience and kindness — this summer I had occasion to see something of it. I intend to write and thank her myself, but in the meantime please tell her how impressed I was with the way she handles Clémence. I thought it not only compassionate in the extreme but skilful and shrewd, because she really knows how to get around our Clémence, no doubt about it.

Yes, I was back at Petite-Rivière-Saint-François for two more weeks after returning from Manitoba. I've been back in Quebec City for ten days now, in an apartment that's clean and tidy at last, which lifts my spirits greatly.

Marcel is well. He was delighted with the hoard of news I brought back from the West, and sends you his best and most affectionate regards.

A big, affectionate hug,

Gabrielle

[Quebec,] December 6, 1958

Ma chère petite soeur,
Remember the lovely portrait of me taken in your arms when I was perhaps two years old, and you probably thirteen[37]? You're holding an arm gently around me, and though I have a serious little face, a bit solemn, sickly-looking, I seem happy to be close to you. We're both wearing our best dresses, all white — or very pale in any event — and the expression on your face is rather tense, dynamic and sorrowful both at once, as though you were already feeling a vocation of renouncement. I've always loved that photograph. Well, Anna had an enlargement made and sent it to me. We found a little old oval frame for it, which I regilded with a special paint. I have it hanging on my wall, and every time I pass by, my eyes rest on those children that we were, you and I, and I feel my heart swell gently with emotion, neither sadness nor cheerfulness but something combining the two, perhaps. In any event, it's a really beautiful reminder of you.

Anna began writing to me again some time ago, which pleases me greatly. Just recently I sent her some money to distribute around the family for me. I asked her to give you $5.00, thinking you'd rather have this little sum for taxi fare than something else — I hope your thoughts match mine on this. I imagine you'll visit Anna during the holidays. Give her a big hug from me and tell her I asked you to, and give Albert[38] one as well, with the same message. From her letters, Clémence seems completely changed — for the better. She seems to want to read, thanks me for the magazines I've sent her, takes the vitamins I've sent her too, and is generally showing an interest in life that she was far from having this summer. I'm so happy about it, so happy indeed about even the smallest pleasure our Clémence is able to feel. It must be that better food, vitamins, and also the attention she's been getting from you and Adèle are all helping her regain her strength. In her last letter, Anna mentioned that you were completely wrapped up in rehearsals with your pupils. Best wishes for your customary success, and in all your activities, you dear little bundle of energy. As for me, this autumn I've been tired beyond words, owing partly to thyroid deficiency as usual. How tired I am of feeling tired almost all the time, if I may put it that way! However, I think I've touched bottom and will now begin to regain some energy. Sunshine would do me the most good. I think I must have been born to live in sunny climes. And how about you, dear skinny little thing? It's not in your nature to spare yourself, but do try whenever you can. Marcel sends you his most affectionate wishes for a perfect Christmas and a New Year of peace and happiness. And so do I with all my heart, my dear little sister. If Maman is still able to watch you from above, I think your life here on earth must be a joy to her eyes.

A big, fond hug to you, wishing you all the happiness your heart desires.

Gabrielle

Quebec City, December 4, 1959

Ma chère petite soeur,
It's high time, or almost, that I wrote you my Christmas letter. We tend to grouch at times about the duties and obligations of the festive season — cards to send, presents, greetings that are always the same and repeated a hundred times over — and there's no doubt that we get into ruts of conventional exchanges that have little to do with what Christmas really means. Not that there isn't a good side to some of these customs, like having to write to one's little sister, for example, especially when it's such a pleasure.

When both of us were having to worry all the time about Clémence, there was a good side to that too because we used to write more often. At the right time and place nearly everything has a good side, I suppose.

I've sent Anna a little money including ten dollars for you, which I imagine you can use for taxis when you go to see Anna, picking up Clémence on the way. So my small present will be travelling familiar streets and taking part in the pleasure you'll all have at being together. Always, when Christmastime comes — and it must be the same for you — I drift back to the past, to Deschambault Street and our loved ones now departed. Yesterday I was reading a beautiful thought of General de Gaulle's in the last volume of his *Memoirs*, which is just out, and which I recommend, by the way; it's a long time since anyone wrote such beautiful French. You'd have to go back to Chateaubriand or Sainte-Beuve for such style, or further still for such content. Anyway, somewhere in the book de Gaulle says this: "In the tumult of events and men, solitude has been my temptation. Nowadays it is my friend." And further on: "As age overtakes me, I feel closer to nature." You could say the same for the past, which really does come close when age overtakes us, doesn't it? So it's natural that you should turn up often in my thoughts, and I keep remembering you the way you were in the little convent parlour in Kenora[39], for instance, when you recited with such feeling for Marcel and me. We leave behind so many different people who once were us, each succeeded by another. But I think you'll soon be saying, That's my Gabrielle, waxing philosophic again! There's some truth in it. This time of year lends itself to philosophizing, and to growing old. But don't you worry, there's plenty of youth in me yet and I hope I'll keep it for a long time to come. How about you, dear little sister whose face has yet to wrinkle or sag? Are you reasonably well this winter? I hope there's been no recurrence of the pain in your leg. And what about your teaching? How hard you work! How hard you've worked all your life! Me too, though very differently. Will you be able to go and see Anna during your Christmas holidays? Not long ago I received another letter from her in which she sounds quite alert, suggesting that her health must still be holding up, for which I'm thankful. But imagine our poor Adèle in France! She was right to go, I think, and I approve of her going, but I can't hold back a shudder when I think how out of her element she must be sometimes, she has such difficulty adapting to others, and the French are so difficult to adapt to! She should have had an experience like this when she was much younger — she might have learned some flexibility, which she so sorely lacks.

Marcel is well, working diligently and apparently happy — and who wouldn't be, having the felicity of living with me, say I with a smile, as you can no doubt imagine. He may go west at Christmas, though it's not certain yet.

A big, affectionate hug to you, my dear little sister, wishing you those things which in truth you have already, but in greater abundance, together with unfailing good health.

Gabrielle

Quebec City, June 23, 1960

Ma chère petite soeur,
I came home from a brief car trip to the Cape Cod region on the American coast to find your sweet, affectionate, and cheery letter waiting. How your letters always lift my spirits! Is this because you know how to see the encouraging side of life? Is it because your own heart is so crystal clear? In any event, while I read your letters I'm in repose, like the seagulls I've seen in repose on the sea among the waves. They let themselves be cradled unendingly there, specks on the ocean, seeming content with life. At the moment I'm getting us ready to leave very shortly for Petite-Rivière, where we'll spend the whole month of July. So it will be difficult for me to meet Sister Marie-Grégoire if she's only going to be in Quebec City in July. I might be able to meet her in August. Anyway, I'm keeping the address you sent me and I'll see what I can do. I'd already heard about the death of Monseigneur Deschambault[40], which grieved me very much. Besides the fact that he married us, I'd received several particularly touching letters from him. I had an almost daughterly affection for him, I suppose, and admired him for his great open-mindedness and humanity.

All you tell me about Clémence, Anna, Albert, and Adèle cheers me enormously. I'd give almost anything in the world for them to have all the happiness possible. To have you write me that you found them all in fairly good health and pretty cheerful makes me feel infinitely better. Particularly my dear Clémence. I so love to hear that she's talkative, sprightly and chirping like a cricket, and taking an interest in things; at such times she's as happy as a child — and seeing her this way touches and delights me as much as seeing a child laugh and express happiness.

As I read your letter I was eager to hear that you were going to the lake on holiday, because I know what deep, exquisite pleasure you take in this, what tenderness you feel for God's world — trees, water, sky, the murmur of waves, the rustling of leaves — all the infinitely mysterious side of creation, which is wonderfully sweet, but also harsh, for there too, if you look closely, you see conflict and the struggle for life. Now that I have a bit of a garden, I see how many enemies of all kinds there are for anything that lives; the smallest flower, the most graceful tree, a bird, a fly, etc. What seems to us at first so peaceful and calm is in truth subject to merciless laws of nature — which is as it should be, no doubt.

But like a tired seagull, take your repose, contemplate the beautiful liquid horizon, see and admire the splendour of it all, rebuild your strength, and perhaps you'll write me one of your most lyrical holiday letters, one of those in which I best hear the beating of your nature-lover's heart, one that lets me share your pleasure too. Perhaps it's through our delight in summer and holidays that we're more united now than ever — you, I, and Maman, whose heart was also in tune with the voices of nature; and Papa too, with his love of roses. Poor old soul, nowadays when I picture him he's almost always in his little garden, tending his roses; or digging in a small flowerbed behind the house and finding an earthworm and holding it out to a robin following on his heels. You know, it's true that whenever he dug in the garden there was always a robin nearby, hoping for a handout, I think, and Papa pretended that from one year to the next it was always the same robin. This is the way I almost always remember him these days. What a sweet image, don't you think? — yet really so like him[41].

So do try to have the happiest and most restful of holidays.

Marcel sends you many friendly greetings. He too read and loved your letter. We both wish you a fine end to the school year and an enjoyable summer.

Much love,

Gabrielle

Quebec, November 26, 1960

Ma chère petite soeur,
Here's a little cheque for you so you can take a taxi all the way when you go to see Anna or Clémence. I suspect that this is still what you'd like most, and it makes me happy to play a little part in the family gatherings that are brightened so by your kindness and gaiety, and that I'd love to be part of in person. I know how much pleasure they give Clémence and Anna, and you too, of course. I hope you'll have an opportunity to spend at least a few hours together at Christmas or the New Year. I've sent Clémence a dress for these occasions. I hope that it suits her and she likes it. It's rather difficult to choose this kind of thing for someone else, however well you know them. Anyway, I decided on something simple, warm and not too fitted, so now let's hope Clémence will at least feel like trying it on.

Sometimes I envy you, not having to bother with all the little chores like going to the hairdresser and shopping for a dress or hat, not such terribly onerous chores, true enough, but they eat into one's time all the same. I've been thinking of you often these days, wondering if you're still as well as you were, whether your teaching isn't too tiring and you aren't wearing yourself out in your great desire to do things well. Because I know you, you're so valiant, too valiant for your own good.

Did you know that Sister Marie-Grégoire[42] has finished her thesis on me? She sent it to me — it's a magnificent piece of work, very serious, very complete. She finally came to see me —just after receiving the Prix Champlain for her book, *Pointe-aux-coques* — and I found her extremely amusing,bubbling over with vitality, very sharp; and she loves my books, especially *Street of Riches*, to an exorbitant degree. In short, she's quite an extraordinary person. I've read her novel, *Pointe-aux-coques*, which she also sent me, and upon my word I think it's singularly good. She also writes plays, so she must be quite a remarkable figure in her convent. Would you like to read her book? It's about life among the Acadians. If you would, I'd be glad to send it to you. I was particularly touched when she told me she had walked down Deschambault Street half expecting to meet Christine and the other characters. Recently, on the program *Arts et Lettres*, Radio-Canada broadcast an extensive three-part study on my books by four learned people, a sociologist, an academic, a critic, etc. Robert Gadouas read passages from the books. I myself was only able to see the third part, since *Arts et Lettres* wasn't on the Quebec City schedule at the beginning of the season. Personally I would never have said anything, but so many people in Quebec City complained and peppered Radio-Canada with letters of protest that it was decided finally to put the program on the schedule, but by then all but the last of the series on me were over. I'm telling you all this because I think it will amuse you and tickle your pride in me — your only fault — a *petit velours* as they used to say, a minor self-indulgence.

Marcel is well. I'm sort of fair to middling, though reasonably well on balance. Marcel is very fond of his little sister Léon and sends her an affectionate, big-brotherly hug.

If you're with Clémence, Anna, Albert, and the others at Christmastime, give them a big warm hug from us both.

My fondest love to you, and do have a happy, radiant, and splendid Christmas.

Gabrielle

1961 — 1963

Quebec City, February 21, 1961

Ma chère petite soeur,
I already owed you a letter of thanks for your lovely Christmas present, the box of writing paper. I'm going to use it to answer my "fan" mail, of which I'm getting quite a lot since I appeared on *Premier Plan.*[43] Your latest letter, which came this morning, brought me out of my torpor, inspired a measure of shame, and set me to writing you at last. I'm relieved that you were so pleased with the interview. I confess it scared me to death. It's so irrevocable; once you've said something, not a word can be taken back. I was afraid I'd be led into saying something I'd regret, out of stage fright. As I wrote to Anna, it turned out that Maman must have been supporting me, because once I got started I stopped worrying and talked as naturally as could be — and without seeming too nervous, didn't you think? Of course, I was in good hands with Judith Jasmin, who manages to put me at ease any time I see her. Besides being so warm and understanding, she's exceptionally intelligent and professional — and that's important, I assure you. With someone less skilled than she, you can be faced with questions that are wishy-washy or phrased so badly they don't arouse any desire to answer. Judith was delighted with the interview — and I'm as pleased for her as for myself. Still, it was pretty unnerving, I can tell you, to appear on a program that has had guests like Montherlant, Mauriac, Giono, Maurois, Cocteau, and, recently, Marcel Pagnol. My worst fear was that I might drag down the standards of the program. Now that it's over, I'm relieved more than anything else. I wouldn't do it again tomorrow, but

I'm glad now to have had the experience, which could stand me in good stead. It's rather extraordinary to be able to see and hear yourself the way others may see you. It lets you see clearly what you could do to improve. But my strongest feeling was one of surprise. Half the time I couldn't really believe that I was that person Judith was interviewing.

I sent some Equanil to Anna at once, this very day. Like you, I'm much afraid that moving is going to be a terrible shock to those two, and since I heard they were going to leave their house I've had a feeling that neither one of them will long survive the stress[44]. I hope I'm wrong, but after your letter and Anna's last letter I'm increasingly uneasy. Poor dear Anna, what a long, hard struggle indeed, only to end up having to part with the little place that was their own, don't you agree? And all of us have been so fond of it, in these past years the closest thing to a home, isn't it? I hate to see it fall into strangers' hands. All the same, I think Albert's right to sell the house and wind up his business. It's a good thing you're there to comfort Anna; go and see her as often as you can. I'm about to send a little money to Clémence for taxi fare. Don't hesitate to take some for that purpose yourself out of what I'm going to give Clémence.

If you're talking to Anna on the phone, tell her that I'm almost as pleased with the message you passed on as with a letter, and that I'll write her again soon, and hope she'll get all the rest she can and not worry about answering unless she really has an urge to, and is strong enough. Marcel sends his best to you, Clémence, Anna, and the rest.

Much love,

Gabrielle

My regards to Sister Diomède.

Quebec City, May 22, 1961

Chère petite soeur,
Here I am, about to try and comfort you with mere words when I so wish I were with you, Anna, Clémence, and also Antonia and her daughters[45]. I'm sure you can imagine what a state I was in coming back to Quebec City, and even more when I received the telegram from Lucille. I had been hoping despite all. I know from my own heartache what pain there must be in your heart, dear little sister, and how tired you must be after running from this one to that, helping and supporting. Still, it's good to be able to fly to someone's help, isn't it?

At least I saw Germain and talked to him. He opened those blue eyes of his, recognized me, even smiled — with pleasure to see me — and that's comforting in a way, though I'm so sorry not to have stayed. Now I simply can't come back for the funeral. Tell yourself that Marcel and I will be there in our thoughts, as close as close can be to you all.

My grief makes it possible for me to feel yours and Antonia's, Lucille's and Yolande's. I'm praying with you and send a big tender hug to each of you.

Gabrielle

Petite-Rivière-Saint-François, July 24, 1961

Ma chère petite soeur,
I'm beginning my "summer" letter for you, if I can call it that, just as I suppose you'll be writing me one when you've had a few weeks of holiday. Will it be at Camp Morton[46] as usual? Beside your beautiful, beloved lake? I hope it will, so you'll rediscover the sweet joys that swell your heart and soul whenever you're in the midst of nature. How you must have yearned for freedom at times in your convent! But then, if you hadn't partly renounced it, would it have such appeal for you now?

You should see Marcel's little flower garden, an orgy of bright, enchanting colours, all mixed up together as in small European gardens — there used to be some that were this way in Saint-Boniface, do you remember? One, if I recall correctly, surrounded a squat little house, though I don't remember what street it was on. Anyway, it must surely have belonged to someone French — or Belgian. In Marcel's garden beside the sea, almost all the flowers are mixed together, combining their colours and waving gaily in the wind. This year we have magnificent delphiniums of such a soft blue they're extraordinary; to one side are some beautiful red poppies; and miniature carnations smelling so sweet. And the roses, the roses! They always make me think of our poor old father who tended his roses so faithfully. A Chinese proverb says, If you want a day of happiness, buy a bottle of wine and get drunk; if you want a week of happiness, get married; if you want a whole life of happiness, plant a garden. There's some truth in that, don't you think?

Two weeks from now at the latest I must go back to Quebec City to finish packing for the trip[47]. We leave on September 2 and come back on October 2. I've had a lot of trips this year, some lovely and others — at least my short stay in Manitoba — unforgettably sad. I still keep seeing Germain's drawn face, the one we both saw in the hospital. But thank God we saw him and he recognized us and smiled at us. I take comfort from this now. And the grief, the anguish we shared, precisely because we shared it together, today has softened to a kind of tenderness among us.

Oh, do try to rest well this summer after all the emotion, fatigue, and work. I wrote to Clémence not long ago. I'm going to write to Anna. Is she still at Léontine's[48]? How is she?

Fond hugs from Marcel and me,

Gabrielle

My very best regards to Sister Malvina — by now almost a sister by blood — to Sister Diomède, dear soul, and to Sister Superior.

Quebec City, October 5, 1961

Ma chère petite soeur,
We've been home since the 2nd of this month and I'm anxious to tell you about our trip and send you a tiny thing I picked out for you at Mistra, an ancient, bygone Byzantine city perched on a hilltop, an incomparable site where the only inhabitants, living ones, are a few Orthodox nuns (there's only one community for women in the Orthodox Church, by the way) who look after the ruins and a small restored monastery, where they do needlework and make icons like the one I'm sending you. I would have liked to send you an old one — they're superb — but the most modest are worth hundreds of dollars, can you imagine? This one I'm sending will give you some idea of Byzantine art; very hieratical, very stylized. For Anna I'm sending a small paper knife that I bought for her in Istanbul, where we stopped for only a day. There's another paper knife for Clémence. Would you attend to passing them on? I could only bring very small things because we were travelling by air and the baggage weight is very limited.

I thought of you often during this trip — every time I stood before some marvellous site with its splendrous monuments of Greek antiquity. How you would love to see these things, some almost intact after so many centuries! I'd need pages and pages to express the emotion, the intellectual pleasure, the boundless admiration, the wonder and astonishment, all the things you feel when you look at the Parthenon, for example, the small temple of the wingless Athena, or the temple of the god Vulcan. The magic of these places comes from the exquisite harmony created by the stone, the sky, and the magnificent surroundings. You begin to understand how the Hellenic period, its culture and thinking, have influenced us so strongly, though we're not always aware of it. There, a great many expressions that have become part of our everyday language, that we use unconsciously, come suddenly to light and take on their full significance. At Olympia, playground of the gods according to the ancients, an aristocratic serenity reigns, making you think of the familiar old expression "an Olympian calm", and you discover how very appropriate it is.

Delphi, where the ancient Greeks went to consult the oracles, is another awe-inspiring place. Greek mythology, which used to rather bore me, fascinates me now. After all, it was a quest for the divine and the absolute.

We saw the famous theatre of Epidaurus, a hemisphere with 55 tiers of stone seats and 155 steps; its acoustics are so perfect that from the highest tier you can hear a person's breathing down on the stage. Here, where Aeschylus, Euripides, and Sophocles were played by the ancients, they are still played today. Maria Callas sang there recently. These places are so filled with history, memories, and greatness that you find far, far more in them than you ever expected.

It was an exhausting trip, of course. We did part of it by bus, in a group with a guide, and another part by ship on a cruise, from one island to another — there are hundreds of them: the Cyclades, the Sporades, the Dodecanese. We touched land at Rhodes, Crete, Mikonos, and Delos, the presumed birthplace of the god Apollo. They are all beautiful beyond words. Later, I'll try to describe it all for you as best I can, once I've sorted out and put some order in my own impressions — they're pretty jumbled at present. In only a month it's really almost too much to take in. Each time there's something to see you're sorry to have to do it so fast.

I'm finding plenty here that's overdue or neglected, as you can imagine. But my book *The Hidden Mountain* will finally be out very shortly[49]. You'll get a copy, of course, and so will Anna and Clémence. I'm dying to have a word from you. During the trip there were times when all of a sudden I was terribly worried about you all, and many occasions when I wished you were sharing the delight and enchantment of discovering Greece — the old and also the new, the modern with its incomparable sky, great harsh mountains, vineyards, olive orchards in the valleys, little snow-white villages; it's all beautiful, dignified, proud; everything there is good except perhaps the olive-oil cooking, which is rather tasteless. I was wary of it but it didn't make me sick because I paid attention and avoided anything that looked too greasy.

Give Anna, Clémence, Albert, and the rest a hug from us. I'll be writing them all before long. Hope to hear from you soon.

Much love,

Gabrielle

Quebec City, December 3, 1961

Ma chère petite soeur,
Since I'm not sure of Yolande's address in Winnipeg, I'm sending you a cheque for $50.00 so you can pass it on to her. It's our present, Marcel's and mine, for her wedding to Jean[50]. I'm sending you $10.00 to help pay your taxi fare when you go visiting Anna and Clémence. I imagine Yolande can come and pick up her cheque at the convent, or you can send it to her by mail. I wouldn't want this to tire you or be a bother.

How are you? I've been worried about you these last few days, all kinds of things going round in my head. I'm impatient for you to stop teaching full time. I think it's too much for you, you're so thin and you've had so little rest for years. Anyway, I really hope that I'm wrong to worry about you and that you're still my irrepressible, enthusiastic, valiant Dédette. Sometimes I think it's you who most takes after Maman, at least her hardworking, tireless, impetuous side. But don't go overboard, don't push yourself too much. All of us — all Mélina's[51] children — have a tendency to live too much on our nerves. It makes the fire burn bright, true enough, but later we pay for it dearly, don't we?

Dear sister, I have so many good and beautiful wishes in my heart for you for Christmas and the New Year. Or rather, I have one wish that covers everything — that peace of soul of which you have a good measure already. May it grow even more, if that's possible, may it bring light to each day, each moment of your life, and may it shine forth from you to others. This is my cherished wish for you.

I imagine you haven't had much time to write me before the Christmas holidays. That's all right. You have so much to do already and I wouldn't want to put pressure on you for anything in the world. I quite often think of our Christmases of long ago and all the trouble Maman took — you remember — to put the most succulent foods on the table. The effort she made was really close to incredible. The summer kitchen was full of things put there to freeze — it was the freezer of those days — fritters, tourtières, mincemeat tarts. Then there was the turkey, fruitcake, Spanish cream, green salad (greens were so inexpensive then), fruit, nuts, and finally the fudge she was famous for. When I think of the work that went into all this superb fare, all sorts of culinary feats, the recollection gives me almost more pain than pleasure. Yet how happy we were, sitting together around the big family table. And what delight there was in Maman's face to see us all there around that big table. Sometimes I think there's nothing lovelier or more tender in the world than this memory. I pass it on to you, to give you a moment of pleasure mixed with sadness — for the two are inseparable in a way, aren't they?

There now, I've gone and written a long letter that has turned out to be rather doleful, though I began by wanting not to write anything that wouldn't cheer you.

Marcel sends you an affectionate hug and he too wishes you peace, health, and happiness.

I'm still dying to get a line from you.

Much love,

Gabrielle

Quebec City, May 3, 1962

Ma chère petite soeur,
I think you're right, I haven't written you for some time, and hadn't heard from you either since Christmas. So I was enchanted to get your last letter, such a sweet, loving letter as always — despite its rather discouraging news. However, I don't think the little operation Anna must have means anything serious in itself. It must be a question of those small stones that sometimes form in the salivary glands; I have some myself, though they haven't bothered me much yet. Her overall state of health is what is most important, and I have the impression she's not doing much to help it, particularly not eating enough. But what can we do about it? As for Adèle, I've sent Clémence a cheque for $100.00 so that she can send it to her. I don't understand why she insists on staying in Montreal, supposedly to have her eyes seen to. Surely that could be done just as well in Winnipeg or Saint-Boniface. Anyhow, if the money can help her, so much the better.

As for you, my dear sister, I see you're still the doughtiest of the family. You dear, fearless soul! You know, I sometimes think you're the one who has most of Maman's mettle.

Thank you for your kind words about *The Hidden Mountain.* When I was writing this book I didn't think I was doing anything so unusual, but as it turns out there are all kinds of interpretations being drawn from it, some of them pretty outlandish in my opinion. Basically it's rather a simple story. The English translation is finished at last, after much tussling, and has been sent to my American publishers. The translator[52] is the same I've always had. I think we're going to stop after this book. It's a very beautiful translation, very elegant, perhaps more lyrical than the original. English is extraordinarily well suited to this kind of writing, it seems to me. The edition in France will come out soon too[53]. I don't think this book will be a big success — with the general public, I mean. On the other hand, those who like it seem to like it very much — and this kind of success is just as good as the other.

We'll probably spend a month at Petite-Rivière, besides weekends here and there. For the moment, the sky is not inviting. The weather is grey, cold, and miserable, and it's raining constantly. It must be that we had spring too early, because it was nicer in March than it is now. Marcel is well, but what a life! There are days when I barely see him. Fortunately he's got into the habit of taking a month of holiday. We've already started our flowers in boxes on the windowsills. We probably planted the seeds too soon, though; the plants are nearly a foot high. They're a nuisance, all those boxes on the windowsills, but it fascinates us to watch these little living things grow and we're always running over to take a look at them. Each of us wants to be the first to water them —madness! In remembrance of Maman, I've seeded some stocks — you remember how they spread their marvellous scent as evening falls. I imagine you must miss your little garden at Kenora; you used to take such good care of it.

And now my best love to you, wishing you many more years of being just the way you are now. Give my love to Clémence and Anna too — I'll write to them soon.

Gabrielle

Quebec City, August 31, 1962

Ma chère petite soeur,
I was so pleased this morning, when I came home from my stay in Percé, to get fresh news of you through Marcel, who tells me he found you cheerful and looking well. He brought me good news about Clémence too, and all this has reassured me. But I'm worried to hear that Anna is with Adèle. In a tiny little room in Montreal, when it's as hot as this, I don't think it can be very comfortable. I don't have Adèle's address, by the way. She probably doesn't ever want to set eyes on me again. Through Clémence, she even returned the cheque for $100.00 that I had sent her. Nevertheless, next time I'm in Montreal I'll try to see her. It really is too silly to harbour a grudge so long, and why, for heaven's sake! So let me have her address, if you will.

At Percé it was magnificent, but I'm barely home and since I found an avalanche of mail waiting — mostly tiresome stuff — and with it the little problems of so-called civilized life, the happy frame of mind I'd acquired there has begun to fade. How you would love Percé, a place that's wild and sophisticated as well with its good restaurants, good food, good places to stay, and so many charming people to meet. You've probably heard of Bonaventure Island, a bird sanctuary opposite Percé, about a mile away, I think. It's worth going to Percé for this alone. There are gannets, big gulls with yellow heads and astonishing blue eyes, by the thousands. It's estimated that there are probably forty-six thousand of them. They live in nests built on narrow ledges on a high, windswept, spray-drenched cliff and the air is constantly filled with their cries, a sound that's mournful but still beautiful, because it speaks to you in mysterious voices from eternity. And then, Percé itself is adorable from all points of view, with its little art centre, a summer theatre, a bustle of bearded young men who are a bit dishevelled but so full of life. On the beaches I took to hunting for agates, like everyone else, and found some rather good ones. This simple pastime relaxed me to a degree I haven't experienced in a long time. I was a child again, bewitched by pretty pebbles, their shapes and colours, and sometimes their beauty, if a ray of light happened to set one sparkling as I picked it up. Now here I am, far removed from all that, alas — it isn't easy to keep the sheer enchantment of such a holiday alive in one's memory. You too have tasted such pleasure, I've recognized it in the tone of your holiday letters, the ones I call "summer letters from my sister who's bursting with love and oneness with the universe". Don't ever lose that vibrance of yours, or stop being happy with the wind, the sky, plants, birds, lakes, and all the things that tell us something about the state of our souls.

Forgive me for this rather ecstatic, somewhat rambling letter. I couldn't write to anyone else in this way. I think you can understand what I'm saying, remembering your own emotion of your times at the little cottage overlooking the lake.

Have a good, rewarding, and not too tiring year, and please, please don't take on any more than the little strength you have permits.

My fondest love to you,

Gabrielle

Quebec City, November 26, 1962

Ma chère petite soeur,

A few weeks ago, after a long eclipse, Anna suddenly began writing to me again. I've received five or six letters in quick succession. Although she speaks of a variety of ills, her morale seems good and the tone of her letters even seems to indicate that she's calmer than she was before. I think this good news can't help but reassure you. After Christmas she may go again to be with Adèle, who keeps asking her to. That's if she feels strong enough, she tells me, and of course she may not. But perhaps you've heard all this directly from her. I've also had a charming letter from Yolande, with a photograph of her beautiful baby. I've just written to her in France so that she'll get it when she arrives. She's at that wonderful age where you adapt easily to everything. Still, it's a very long step from Manitoba to France, and I'd like to help make it a little less bewildering for her. I'm delighted that she's lucky enough to have the experience of living in France for a time. It can't fail to have a profound effect on her and, I imagine, incline her even more towards French, since she already has a taste for the language and culture.

Unlike Lucille, unfortunately. We were rather pained, Marcel and I, to see that Lucille doesn't even speak French to her children. Not that I'm casting a stone at her. I know full well how difficult it is to keep up the struggle in a milieu that's as completely English as hers.

So there's my news, and here's some more: Eliane and Laurent Jubinville[54] paid us a surprise visit about two weeks ago. You probably know that two of their daughters are in Quebec City: Monique, who teaches English in several schools there, and Céline, who is a student at l'Université Laval. I found Eliane exactly the way she was when we were both young; full of fun, easygoing; even her rather coarse, throaty laugh hasn't changed. You'd think you were listening to a pigeon. I enjoyed the visit enormously, I don't really know why. I suppose she wakened a thousand memories for me of those happy times I had at Uncle Excide's farm as a child, then as a teenager. For me, those days are made of indescribable memories. Everything about them glows, and they're full of wonderful tenderness and charm. They make me think of Maman at her happiest, because, as you remember, she really loved those holidays at the farm; they must have taken her back to her own roots on the land. Anyway, talking about all this with Eliane, I was almost blissfully happy for a full hour. Miraculous, isn't it, how memories well up in us in response to a certain voice, a certain stimulus. Though she didn't know it, Eliane's laugh must have been the key that opened those doors to the past for me.

As for me these days, there's little or nothing worth mentioning. Marcel is getting to be very busy, much too busy for my liking. I'd like to be enjoying life with him a bit more, but he seems happy with the way things are and that's the main thing. I'm trying to work on a series of longish stories[55], but I wonder if I'll ever publish them, whether I'll ever publish anything again, I have so little stomach for all the rigmarole involved in publishing, all the time it wastes, all the fatigue it brings. And to tell the truth, although I'm not really unwell, I have to cope almost constantly with being tired. It's not new; I sometimes think I've been tired most of my life. You don't get used to it, either — at least, not completely.

And how are you, dear little sister? Even if you were tired I don't think you'd admit it. You're the most valiant of us all. Still, I'd like to think you allow yourself some rest. You little dynamo, your batteries ought to be quite dead, totally drained after working the way you do, spending your strength like that.

You remember Sister Marie-Grégoire, who wanted so much to meet me and who wrote an excellent thesis on me, and then a first novel, *Pointe-aux-coques*? Well, she's just written another, *On a mangé la dune*[56], which is as delightful as the first. It's still about her little Acadian world, which she depicts charmingly and refreshingly. I may be mistaken, but as I read it I wondered if she hadn't been somewhat influenced by *Street of Riches*, which would be a kind of compliment. *Street of Riches* continues to make a respectable showing, and this year will become a school book. When I began to write, I never dreamed I'd be read in the schools. So it's all quite amazing.

I suppose you see Clémence now and then. I'm worried about her feeling lonely now that Anna's no longer in Manitoba[57].

I enclose my usual little cheque for you to spend on whatever you like, if you're allowed. I'm also going to send you some sweets.

Have a pleasant Christmas, dear sister; may your holidays allow you to ease up a mite, and may the love of God that burns in you remain steadfast. My kind regards to your companions in religious life. Marcel sends you an affectionate, brotherly hug. Hope to hear from you soon.

Gabrielle

Quebec City, January 20, 1963

Ma chère petite soeur,
I received your lovely little apron, which I'll use without fail when I'm at Petite-Rivière. I've also just received your sweet letter. First of all, don't worry, I don't bear Adèle any kind of grudge; I know too well how bitterness gnaws at one, how much harm it does. I was just hurt, which I can't hide, that she has accused me of intentions towards her that I certainly never had. As for helping her financially, I'll do so the minute she wants me to.

I've just had all my lower teeth out because I was having very painful abscesses. What I find hardest is eating. How on earth does poor Clémence manage? I assure you, the little aches and pains we suffer help us know how others feel. But to be truthful, having your teeth out isn't really so dreadful.

I was delighted with the account of the little party in honour of you and your companions. A lovely thing about you nuns is the way you've kept the childhood gift of pleasure and wonder. I think I expressed something of this in my story "Sister Finance"[58]. Sister M. G. was the model I began with, of course. In other respects, the story I tell is almost entirely invented. However, it's invented in a way that expresses the truth better than reality does. I'm glad you like it.

I've just received a rather laconic letter from Clémence. She misses Anna, I think. Luckily she still has you. She tells me about your visits with an artless joy that lets me sense how much they mean to her. Poor little Clémence, how often my heart aches to think of the way she lives, her curious lot in life.

As for you, do try to take care of yourself. I'd like to see you scale down your activities and take more rest. Marcel and I both send our affectionate regards. Marcel always loves to read your letters.

Gabrielle

I'm delighted to hear about your diploma; my heartiest congratulations.

Quebec City, June 25, 1963

Ma chère petite soeur,

I don't remember whether I've answered the delightful letter you wrote when you returned from your trip to the Pacific coast[59]. In any event, I must tell you that your description of the ocean and the magnificent

Rockies enchanted me. It's a great joy to be able to contribute to someone's pleasure, and I felt as I read your letter that I might have had something to do with the thrill and deep emotion you felt on discovering those noble landscapes. Such hunger and adoration for nature is part of us, we children of Mina[60], and I understand so well your excitement at seeing its most magnificent spectacles. I've had times when I've felt the same way to see certain of nature's simplest things. Some little country road at twilight, for example, can raise me for a few moments to the strangest and most incomprehensible state of joy.

I'm sending you enclosed a cheque for $10. (ten dollars) for pocket money, taxis when you go to see Anna and Clémence. Try to take some good, restful holidays this summer. I hope you'll also go and sit beside the great, beloved lake you so enjoy.

As for me, I'm leaving shortly with Marcel for Petite-Rivière, but this year we'll only be there for a couple of weeks, because Marcel wants to keep two or three weeks of holiday for next autumn. Anyway, I don't think we'll suffer too much from the heat if we have to spend part of the summer in the city, because our new apartment seems much more airy and cool than the old one[61]. You'd think you were in the country because you can see huge trees all around from our windows, and the wind keeps rustling the leaves. I know I'm going to like it here eventually, now that I'm beginning to get used to it. However, it's going to take a lot more organizing than in our little cubbyhole, where I had everything within reach.

I hope Anna finds a place where she'll be comfortable and content.[62]

Have a nice, restful, pleasant summer, all three of you. My love to you all.

Gabrielle

Paris, September 18, 1963

Ma chère petite soeur,

I've sent you (by ordinary mail) a program of the Féerie de Notre-Dame that I attended last night, surrounded by a huge crowd gathered on the banks of the Seine. In the crowd there were a great many little nuns from Paris and other French cities, and even elsewhere, I imagine. It was touching to see them out so late at night, and afterwards going home in small groups by the Métro. It made me think of you, and I kept imagining your exclamations of amazement to see the Féerie unfold. The word is well chosen; it was certainly that, a glimpse of fairyland. Beautiful voices, the most beautiful in France, telling the story of the cathedral while searchlights played on the great coloured rose window, or the prodigious spire, or the nave or transept. The only ones not entering into the spirit of things were the white pigeons brought here specially, which were supposed to fly up in a cloud when the bells began to ring; rather than play their part, those disobedient pigeons stayed peacefully asleep on ledges or the shoulders of statues, or in the beards of saints.

I think I'll soon be back in Quebec. Ask Anna to forgive me for not having sent her a letter or card. I'll rectify that soon.

This summer, did you get a cheque for $10.00 that I sent you for pocket money?

Say hello to Clémence for me.

Take care of yourself and try to write me very soon.

Affectionately,

Gabrielle

Quebec City, December 7, 1963

Ma chère petite soeur,

Your letter, which I received a while ago, enchanted me. You've always expressed yourself well, but I think your letters are getting more and more interesting, filled with well-chosen expressions which you're using with increasing subtlety. So you're still hard at work. I'm glad for you since you seem to be so happy with it. I telephoned Monique Jubinville[63] to tell her that her young sister is one of your pupils, and how highly you think of her. Monique was touched. Marcel and I have just returned from a little trip to Montreal. That city is now growing at an almost fantastic pace. Quebec is growing too, but at a more tolerable rate, and altogether I like living here better than in a city as huge and hectic as Montreal.

I'm sending you a cheque for $10.00, thinking that this is still what will give you most pleasure since you can spend it as you like, on your little taxi rides or to buy yourself something. What's keeping your community from buying a car? Here, a number of convents have them and it's not unusual to see sisters at the wheel. In Paris this summer, I saw any number of nuns running their errands around town with their own little cars. It must be so convenient.

I hope you're well. Most of all, don't tax your strength.

Have the best Christmas possible and a happy new year.

Much love,

Gabrielle

Quebec City, December 31, 1963

Ma chère petite soeur,
I've received your card and the slippers. They're really lovely; the sister who made them has excellent taste. They'll be most useful; thank you for such a very nice present.

When the holidays come I hope you'll have enough time off to rest well and give Clémence a little attention. Poor soul, she must be lonely since Anna left[64]. At Christmas I had a line from Anna, who doesn't seem at all well. I think she regrets having left for Phoenix now and feels terribly far away. Try to keep each other company, you and Clémence, and when you're together I'll be there with you both in my heart. Try as I may, at this time of year I can't help remembering our lovely festive gatherings when we were sometimes as many as twenty around the family table, doing justice to the feast Maman had spent so much time preparing. There aren't many people today who take the pains she did to provide a banquet like that. I remember best of all those marvellous Spanish creams, those rather than the tourtières, perhaps because I never could eat food as heavy as that. How happy it made her to see us eating like horses!

Yolande too sent me a card, with a photo of our babykins. That little Gisèle quite won my heart when I saw her for the first time this summer in her little pink dress, her golden hair shining in the sun. She looks even more beautiful now, and her character, her personality, seems to be asserting itself already, judging by her saucy little smile. I hope Yolande finds the time to take her to see you. A little child of that age is such an enchanting sight.

We're having a happy, peaceful holiday season. Marcel has had the flu, but he's recovering well and is enjoying being able to rest at home for a few days, relaxing, reading, watching T.V. Television is his main relaxation. I even think he overdoes it; while you see good things on television, you see and hear a lot that's mediocre, too. I invited the daughter of my friend Paula Sumner, now Madame Bougearel[65], to spend Christmas with us — her daughter Monique who is eighteen. It was such a pleasure for us both to have her with us for three days. Marcel and I don't know many young people, have rather forgotten what it is to be young, perhaps; so the presence of this adorable child made us feel young and gay again. She's very mature for her age, in fact, because she's been in many countries, travelled since she was born, so to speak, and studied several years in France, all of which has given her a strong, most engaging personality. And she speaks the most beautiful French. She seemed delighted to be with us as well, telling me she felt as though she were part of the family, because all her life she had heard her mother speak so warmly of us.

That's all the news I have. I don't have anything more to tell you except that it's extremely cold these days, ten, fifteen, even twenty below zero. It's hard to take, yet the sun is shining and you can't say it's depressing weather. There's even a kind of savage splendour in days like this, vivid white snow under a piercing blue sky.

Are you dressed well enough for this kind of cold? I've always thought you little sisters don't put enough on in winter. You ought to be wearing big warm furs, it seems to me.

Marcel sends his best wishes.

A big, very affectionate hug from us both.

Gabrielle

I forgot to tell you that Monique Bougearel is in Montreal, where she's been sent to study by her parents, who are still in Durban, South Africa but are approaching the end of their posting and will be moving next to France . . . or perhaps Canada.

1964 — 1965

Quebec City, January 7, 1964

Ma chère petite soeur,

Clémence has had a real inspiration and you too were inspired to pass it on to me. At first I didn't think it would be possible for me to leave for Phoenix at this time, but after rereading Fernand's letter[66] I felt I was being called to go to our poor Anna, representing us all, as you say. So I'm leaving the day after tomorrow and will write you as soon as I've seen Anna. It's very upsetting making a last-minute decision and setting off on a trip like this, but I'm counting on your kind prayers to help and strengthen me. You're the one who would really be the most help there. I thought briefly of offering you a ticket, but would you have been free to leave? And how would you manage once you were there? Anyway, I'll pass on some news as soon as possible. Meanwhile, thank you in advance for your prayers and the moral support you never fail to give me.

Ever so much love,

Gabrielle

Phoenix, January 11, 1964

Ma chère petite soeur,
I saw Anna when I arrived, for just a few minutes. What a sad sight she is! She has wasted away to skin and bone, but her morale is good. Rest assured, she has received the sacraments and will die with her soul in peace. When that will be, no one dares predict, but I don't think it can be long. I gave her your message of love, and Clémence's, and she smiled. Léontine told me that was the first time she had seen her smile in ages. I think they're going to arrange for her not to suffer too much. She gets injections to calm her, but she's perfectly lucid none the less. Talking tires her terribly, so we can't stay with her more than a few minutes. I'll go back tomorrow with Paul, who has arrived with Malvina. We'll probably telephone Gilles today and have him come[67].

We mustn't regret that Anna's dying here. It's beautiful, the sky is clear and the sun shines bright and cheerful. Léontine tells me that Anna was happy with it all until she went into hospital.

In my opinion her cancer must have spread all through her, and she must have a strong constitution to have fought it so long.

We have your prayers if not your comforting presence, and we all sense you close to us and feel the better for it.

I'll write you again shortly.

Much love,

Gabrielle

Desert Hills Hotel, Phoenix, January 13, 1964

Ma chère petite soeur,
I've been to see Anna two or three times a day since I arrived Friday evening. The following morning I saw a change for the worse, and again the day after. Her condition seems to have stayed about the same since. However, I don't think it's possible for her to last much longer because

she's only being fed through her veins. The cancer is generalized and has attacked her liver, stomach, and probably other organs too. Still, she's not in pain, because they're keeping her under sedation. So far she has remained lucid, and I've been able to talk to her and she has been answering a little, though what she's saying is less and less clear. It's hard to watch her being slowly consumed like this. She's not afraid of death any more, tells me she wants it, in fact, and I've done my best to give her confidence in the beyond. As a comfort, I left Maman's little old rosary in her hands, the one you took from Maman's hands when she was resting in her coffin and gave to me. Since then I've never been without it, and several times in my life it has been a great comfort to me. Anna seemed pleased to have it. It's dreadful to admit this, perhaps, but we've come to the point where we hope she'll die as soon as possible, since this is what she wants and we are exhausted. Paul is a pitiful sight. I've always known him to be an extremely sensitive boy; if he weren't he wouldn't have built himself such a hard shell. Gilles may not come. We spoke to him by telephone and he was going to come, but now he's not sure. It's true that it's a very expensive trip. And Anna has reached the point where I really don't think she cares much about anything here on earth.

I'll count on you to pass the news on to Clémence without upsetting her too much, and to Adèle, if you think it right.

Much love,

Gabrielle

Desert Hills Hotel, Phoenix, Monday January 20, 1964

Ma chère petite soeur,

As I told you, Adèle, and Marcel by telegram, Anna died yesterday morning, the 19th, at 9:15. They had called us from the hospital shortly before, and she had just drawn her last breath when we arrived at her bedside, Fernand, Léontine, and I, and also Gilles, who had arrived

Friday afternoon. She had been in a semi-comatose state for twenty-four hours, but on Friday she was still lucid although extremely weak, and we were each able to talk to her a little. Since I've been here, not a day has gone by that I haven't seen her, and most days I've been to see her three times. We only went for very short little visits, because talking tired her terribly. Last Wednesday she received communion, and it was time, because after that she couldn't really keep food down. We were able to follow the horrible progress of the illness step by step, so to speak, with the appearance of jaundice, then the invasion of more or less all her organs by the cancer, and it was a spectacle that I don't think I will ever be able to erase from my mind. But she didn't suffer, or so it seemed, except from weakness and distress. At least, that's what she told me each time I asked if she was in pain. Apparently the morphine did soothe the pain almost completely. I did my best to calm her anxiety about death, but you would certainly have succeeded better than I. It's odd, but for two days while she was still lucid she seemed reconciled to the thought of death, telling me she hoped it would come soon and was afraid of dragging on. Then later she seemed surprised, stunned, to think she had been condemned, but I think this was an effect of the morphine. On Saturday morning she slipped into a semi-comatose state and never came out. Saturday, the day before she died, we saw her three times in the course of the day. She had said something to her nurse that morning, then never talked afterwards and seemed not to be conscious. Paul had to leave Friday morning and so was not there when she died, but he had paid everything before leaving; he had also hired two private nurses for her, so right to the end she never lacked for care, and had all possible spiritual help as well.

We will bury her tomorrow, Tuesday, in a cemetery on the outskirts of the city of Phoenix, under a sky that is always blue, in a climate where the weather is always fine, in a strange land of strange and wonderful trees, far away from where she lived, though I think she was consoled by the thought that she would be resting in ground warmed by an ardent sun. She had been happy here until about six weeks ago, marvelling to see orange, date, and pepper trees wherever she turned, besides trees as common here as at home, like birches, spruces, and poplars. Léontine has been extraordinarily good to her, caring for her with untiring devotion. All of us, I think, have done our best to help her cross the bridge from life to death. The priest of Fernand's parish, a kind

Franciscan father, a priest of the poor, will celebrate the last rites.

This morning we received your letter and Rodolphe's[68], both too late as you can see. I couldn't even read your previous letter to her, because she was already in a semi-conscious state when it arrived. However, I was able to read her Adèle's letter, which arrived a few days earlier. She seemed pleased when I talked to her about you and about the fervent prayers you were saying for her. She resigned herself quickly to the idea that you couldn't come, saying, "It was really to give Bernadette a nice trip and have her see a lovely place that I wanted her to come." She kept calling you "our little saint. . . ." Then I'd take the opportunity to talk about the transferability of merit and the community of saints, trying to have her understand that the merits of some can compensate for the shortcomings of others, and that before God we can borrow these merits and have them credited to our own account. I tried to make these weighty, mysterious things understandable for a mind weakened by illness and morphine, and it was very difficult for me because this is the first time in my life that I've tried to help a dying person. I hope I didn't shrink too much from the task.

In grief and tenderness, my love to you, my dear little sister. I'll probably be home Thursday this week. I telephoned Marcel Saturday evening and he thinks I should stay a few days longer to rest in this warm climate, but I have no heart now to enjoy it and feel terribly out of my element here. Would you please pass on what I've told you to Rodolphe, Adèle, and Clémence. I'll write to Clémence a little later and Léontine will take care of writing to Anna's[69] friends.

Keep as close an eye as possible on Clémence.

Affectionately,

Gabrielle

Desert Hills Hotel, Phoenix, Wednesday January 22, 1964

Ma chère petite soeur,
It's occurred to me that you might like to have an idea of the nursing home where Anna spent her last days on earth. She had a lovely room all to herself, sunny and cheerful and very comfortable, though she didn't really enjoy it, poor thing. I'm enclosing a folder giving some details about this place. Since the Good Samaritan Hospital, where she had been before, couldn't or wouldn't keep her any longer, Fernand had to move her last Tuesday, a week ago today. The trip by ambulance from one hospital to the other was a diversion for her, like a Sunday drive, would you believe it? She marvelled at the trees along the way, palm and orange trees, telling me once again, as she had several times before, that this Phoenix was a wonderful city.

Yesterday at 11:30 we had a graveside ceremony, called a "churchyard ritual" here, or something like that, and the Franciscan father of Fernand's parish officiated. He himself had suggested this, rather than a church service, because there were so few of us, Gilles, Fernand, Léontine, myself, and the three children[70]. But everything was done with such great dignity and restraint that Anna would have approved, I think. It took place under a magnificent sky, on a real summer day. So Anna is resting at St. Francis Cemetery; Fernand tells me he'll try to send you a little photograph of the grave.

The poor fellow leads a very precarious life here and is consumed by worry over the future. It's partly his own fault, perhaps, but you might as well blame a sparrow for what it is. I'm afraid Anna's will is really going to disappoint her children[71], from what she gave me to understand. But it wasn't the time to try and change her mind when I arrived on the scene; she had already been under narcotic sedation for too many weeks.

Anyway, let's hope it works out for the best.

We were touched by a telegram we received from Antonia and Yolande[72]. Please give them our thanks. I sent a telegram to Adèle myself, but nothing more; I'm leaving it to you to tell her what other details you consider appropriate.

I'm sending you two picture postcards from Arizona to give you an idea of the rather strange vegetation in the semi-desert surrounding the city. I've seen the most beautiful sunsets in the world here, with the trees of the desert, those great cactuses, silhouetted against a deep red sky.

Much love,

Gabrielle

I'll be back in Quebec Friday afternoon.

Quebec City, January 30, 1964

Ma chère petite soeur,

Marcel and I were greatly moved by your lovely letter. If I may, I'm going to send it to Fernand and Léontine, who can't fail to find comfort in it too. They really need it, Léontine so exhausted from taking care of Anna for so long, then going to visit her at the hospital almost every day for over a month, Fernand having had so much to do besides his work, getting her into hospital, making sure she had a doctor, arranging to have her taken from the hospital to the nursing home, and then the burial. The poor boy is thin and nervous after all this, and worried about the future for himself and his children. I hope your prayers will help him find a better-paying job and peace of mind.

Don't worry about Maman's little old rosary, I've recovered it. I value it enormously, battered as it is, mended and patched time and again, or *raboudiné* as Maman would say, cobbled up. I think there's something of her life on earth, her courageous spirit, attached to this humble rosary.

Thank you for all your visits to Clémence. I'm sure this is the best way to help her bear her grief. All the same, you must have found it tiring to be running to the home while carrying on all your other activities. Do try to rest now. I'm managing to do so myself at present, and the fine weather reigning in the city, the magic of these winter days when the trees are decked with crystal, helps my heart bear the unrelenting sadness of seeing someone close disappear. It's astonishing that after a shock of this kind we can gradually reawaken to the charms of the world around, and even rejoice in them. It's the way we're made, and just as well, no doubt.

I've received quite a number of mass cards in memory of Anna, which I'm sending on to Fernand and Léontine. They're the ones who have shouldered most of the strain this last while. I'm writing a little note to Clémence, not to tell her the details you've already given her, but so she'll know that I think of her often, and particularly often at present.

You do us all so much good, and it's something you must never forget. You're our one real pillar. Anna was quite right when she asked for you a few days before she died. May you be repaid in love and tenderness for all this.

Much love,

Gabrielle

Quebec City, April 30, 1964

Ma chère petite soeur,
I neglected — I don't quite know how — to send you the small sum enclosed to have some masses said for Anna's soul in Saint-Boniface Church, perhaps, or elsewhere if you prefer, in our name — Marcel's and mine — or the whole family's — as you think best. Will you send me the receipts?

I'll write at more length as soon as I have a little more time. For the moment I'm pretty busy. How are you? How is Clémence? And Adèle? Have you had news from her recently?

Much love,

Gabrielle

P.S. I had some masses said for Anna in Phoenix too, in Fernand and Léontine's parish church. Do you think Adèle needs money, and if so, is there a way we can get some to her?

G.

Petite-Rivière-Saint-François, May 5, 1964

Chère petite soeur,
I just got the enclosed letter from Clémence. Do you think you can step in to keep her from leaving the home and going to live with Adèle? It would be disastrous for both of them, I'm afraid. What a tricky situation, eh? My God, how all this distresses me! Still, if you can't do anything don't be too upset.

Let's pray for them both.

Love,

Gabrielle

Petite-Rivière-Saint-François, July 22, 1964

Ma chère petite soeur,
I received your beautiful letter, so filled with your love of creation that when I read it I couldn't help feeling your exhilaration and seeing and hearing the things that delight you so, the lake, the woods, the sky and clouds, even the constant murmur of wind in your little clump of poplars. I have a similar little wood of birch and poplar saplings which I hear rustling just about all the time, and I love these trees more than any

others because their foliage is so sensitive — so like our own hearts, when you think of it, so easily stirred, so constantly on the alert. You're quite right to see the Lord present in all these things, and indeed he must have made them in order to enchant us, but if you look a little closer at what happens in nature — struggle, conflict, murder — I assure you that you'll see nature's way as merciless and harsh beyond imagining. So to remain untroubled in your love of nature, you'd best not go past the edge of the veranda. All the same, I was entranced by your vibrant description of your two weeks' holiday. How I would love to have you here with us, for a few days at least, beside a spectacle of nature that couldn't fail to enthuse you. Our dear Anna, not long before she died, remarked that you had no equal for helping the rest of us see things we often miss though they're right before our eyes, because with your ardour and exuberance you really *see* them. In any event, she too seemed to have been deeply impressed by the trip to Vancouver, and largely because of you. Without doubt it was one of her happiest experiences in the last years of her life.

Marcel and I are having a lovely, rather lazy summer, lovely in a way that makes you think of the unreality of dreams: no telephone, almost no mail, few or virtually no visitors; after a few weeks you feel yourself slipping into a kind of torpor, which probably has its beneficial side. But it's hard to drag yourself out of this state and face up to all the obligations in our lives, which in fact we create for ourselves, and most of them probably make no sense at all.

So I'm reassured about you. You've had your holiday, regained your strength, communed with the source of your summer happiness. I hope Clémence will also have a bit of a holiday, perhaps at Somerset[73]. I offered to send her to the home at Notre-Dame-de-Lourdes, but she said she didn't feel like going there this year. I know you don't neglect her, but keep your eye on her and I'll be most grateful.

In August I may go and finish up the holidays in the Gaspé, where the air is more salty and sealike, but I'm not certain yet because it hasn't been a particularly nice summer — very humid, rainy, and alternately too hot or too cold. Still,. it's better than no summer at all, though it seems to me that years ago we used to have far more pleasant summers.

Marcel sends you an affectionate hug, as do I. How happy I would be if I could give you a hug in person!

Gabrielle

Quebec City, November 19, 1964

Ma chère petite soeur,
The letter I had from you yesterday gave me such pleasure; first because your letters always delight me; also because this one brought a little piece of news that made me particularly happy. I'm talking about the outing you took Clémence on. I'm sure this is the way to bring her as much happiness as it's possible for her to have in this life. If our old mother is kept informed of our little comings and goings where she is, I think she too must have been delighted with this bright idea of yours. I'm sure our Creator must be pleased with us when he sees us enjoying his creation, and you've never failed in this. In fact, our whole family is quite gifted in this way. One of the last things Anna said to me, when I'd observed that the weather was beautiful that day and the sky was blue and clear, was, "Oh yes, it's a marvellous place." When she had suffered so much it was lovely to hear her express enthusiasm for life in spite of it all.

I'm glad you took the opportunity of Fernand and Léontine's visit to tell them how highly I think of them, of Léontine in particular. Poor little woman, it pains me to look at her too, so exhausted from giving to others, yet much happier than others because of this constant giving of herself. Whatever Fernand's faults, and they're mostly faults of immaturity, I thought and still think that Anna treated him harshly, alas, and I feel for him[74]. So I'm particularly pleased that you made a point of expressing our affection and esteem, because, for all his childishness, he's sensitive to any show of affection. As it happens, Léontine has written me since their return to Phoenix; their means of subsistence there may be precarious but they're happy with the climate and the beauty of the countryside, and I wonder if it isn't they who are right, forgoing security for life under such a friendly sky. I certainly wouldn't say they're wrong, in any event.

You're in pretty good health, you tell me, though a little tired. Not too tired, I hope. For me, though they've never been able to find the cause, fatigue has been more or less a constant companion for many years, and I suppose I should be used to it. It must be a matter of constitution. And yet I look after myself and lead the most sensible life. Recently I spent four days in hospital — the one Marcel's attached to — having a lot of tests. They show that my general condition really isn't bad on the whole, except that I have a high cholesterol level, which means I'll have to go on an even stricter diet, although I'm already pretty restricted on that score. I have some sinusitis too, giving me some facial neuralgia, which isn't unbearable yet, far from it, but if it became so I suppose I'd have to have an operation, and that scares me, I don't know why, because it's only a minor thing. But I hope to get away without it. And as for the cholesterol, there's a new treatment using corn oil — non-saturated fat — which does wonders, it seems. The Nobel Prize for Medicine was won by a young American whose discovery of this may be as important as the discovery of penicillin a few years ago.

I hope you'll forgive all these very tiresome details. I don't know why I'm giving them to you. It's probably because you so regularly ask after my health.

I see that you liked our sister-in-law Julia[75]. There's something most appealing about her. I very much enjoyed my stay with her and Jos, that summer when I went there a year before Jos died. And what beautiful sunsets there were on the prairie! Reds the like of which I've never seen anywhere else, except perhaps in Arizona. Those immense red skies used to delight me so much I'd drop everything when the time came and hurry away down the road towards the west. Julia and Jos, who noticed that I always took off at this hour and discovered why, actually changed the time of the evening meal so there'd be nothing to keep me from being on the road, walking towards the fiery sky; which is why, recalling this small detail, I think of Julia as a most considerate soul. Jos was too, for all his rather rough manner.

Dear you, my letter has grown longer and longer. I'm sending you a modest little money order, perhaps to pay for some taxi rides. You'll also be getting a small box of candies from me and Marcel.

We both send you much love and our best wishes for a Merry Christmas and a good and very happy new year.

Gabrielle

Quebec City, January 5, 1965

Ma chère petite soeur,
Thank you from both me and Marcel for your kind presents and your lovely letter which came this morning. The truth is, I'm always happy to get a letter from you; it never fails to cheer and stimulate me. Among other things, your description of Yolande's visit with her little girl went to my heart. The child is precious indeed, more than other children, to my mind. Perhaps she's especially beautiful and appealing to us because she's our flesh and blood. And then we're getting old, so to our eyes there's nothing more beautiful than the freshness of a life beginning. You remember how Maman used to adore her grandchildren when she was old, and indeed every baby she set eyes on. I'm so happy you had this lovely visit and I envy you a little. But I'll probably get my turn.

As for what you write me about Adèle, I rather suspected as much, and I'm not surprised she misses Anna's letters. I miss them terribly myself. Poor, tragic Anna, she had to die to make us realize that since Maman's death she had in a way taken her place, become in turn the nucleus, the centre and soul of the family. Now there's no one left to really hold us together, and for all the affection we have for each other, it's not entirely the same thing. A piece of the cement that held us together has dropped away. Still, sad as it is, we mustn't encourage Adèle's fantasy about living with Clémence. They're both past the age where they can adapt to living with someone else. I don't mean to say it's not pathetic to see them both alone, but better that — a thousand times better — than having them together and miserable.

I've sent Clémence vitamins but she never says anything about them, so does she even take them? It's an excellent formula, B and C in quantities appropriate for her condition. Try to find out if she still has some, if she takes them and if they're doing her any good, because I've asked her and asked her questions I'd like answers to but she rarely gives me any.

God bless you for your visits to her, and God keep you in good health. I hope your evening of plays was a success as always; how I would have loved to be there! Don't worry too much about my health. My diet has already done me a great deal of good and will surely do more. It's a rather tiresome diet, but I'm getting used to it. I also have sinusitis, and for the moment they're giving me antibiotics, hoping to spare me an operation. All these things are more tiresome than serious.

If you need more money for your visits to Clémence or to buy things for her, don't hesitate to let me know.

Have a very happy year, my dear little sister. Much love from us both,

Gabrielle

Quebec City, February 4, 1965

Chère petite soeur,

You'll probably be surprised to have another letter from me so soon after the last. It's because I'm worried about Adèle. I've just noticed that she hasn't cashed the cheque for $100.00 that I sent her shortly before Christmas. I expected this, to tell the truth. She hasn't let up towards me; it's her way of spiting or punishing me, whichever, and she's found the right way, because it hurts me terribly that she refuses to accept the help I offer in such good faith, however she sees it. But I think she'd accept money coming from you, or for that matter from anyone except me. It's childish, really, but what can we do about it?

On the other hand, I wouldn't want to embarrass you and trouble you by sending you money to give to her. Please tell me what you think of all this and what you'd advise me to do. I'm afraid Adèle sees persecution everywhere and misinterprets everything I've done or said about her. Not that I've never done her any wrong; inevitably, in this life all of us have done each other wrong at some time.

You've had news from her. What kind of news? You told me, of course, about her crazy notion of living with Clémence, which mustn't be encouraged at all costs. It would be disastrous.

On the 19th it will be a year since Anna died. How strange that I have the impression I know and understand her better now than when she was alive. We learn an enormous amount about people when they die. I know now that she was consumed by a need to love and be loved, and that something was preventing her from letting herself go in response to this need. Poor soul, life must have caused her such pain.

And you, dear heart, how are you? Be well, look after yourself, think of me, and pray for us both. Good luck with your plays.

Much love,

Gabrielle

Quebec City, May 22, 1965

Ma chère petite soeur,

You wrote me a very loving and delightful letter and it gave me such pleasure. Now that there are fewer and fewer of us, we children of our little mother Mélina, it's going to be important for us to close ranks and keep in touch by writing fairly often. Almost at the instant your letter was arriving to tell me about the things you've been so busy with — the performance, rehearsals, etc. — and about Pauline Boutal[76], Pauline herself appeared on a brief visit to Quebec City — so very brief, alas —bringing me news of you. Such a happy coincidence. I hardly saw her, as it turned out, but of course even a short visit is so much better than no visit at all.

As for Adèle, I jotted down her bank account number somewhere, Anna having given it to me, but I must have mislaid it. Anyway, I think it would be better if you would agree to deposit the money for her yourself, after getting the number from her, or else send her the enclosed cheque, having endorsed it. This way the pride that I suppose forbids her to accept anything from me wouldn't be wounded. It's a farce, but it doesn't do anyone any harm, after all. However, if you don't like this way of going about it, tell me quite frankly and I'll try to find another way.

I'm impatient to see you get away to the country, breathe the clean air, and relax in the natural surroundings you enjoy so much. When you do, you mustn't forget to write me your usual midsummer letter, the one I'm always eager to get; I think of it as my little sister the nun's summertide hymn.

What a shame I can't hope the same for Clémence, who so loves a little change of scene and the pleasures of the country in summer.

Perhaps you'll find a way to take her on a day's picnic at least, or some other little excursion.

Marcel too was charmed and delighted to see you in February. Since my trip to Arizona, I hear quite often from Léontine and Fernand, whom I've become fond of and who have fine qualities, really. They seem to be fond of me too. We probably shouldn't judge Anna, but I confess I can't understand what possessed her to make such a strange will, leaving a pretty generous share of her money ($1000.00) to cancer research, for example, and quite a large amount to the parish of Saint-Eugène, and to Fernand and Léontine, who are practically in poverty, a wretched little monthly allowance[77]. I would have expected her to leave a little something to Adèle as well, a few hundred dollars, or at least two hundred. In any event, there's nothing to be done about it now, but I feel the same way as Fernand and Léontine, who were terribly disappointed by the will.

I'll stop my letter here, since I've quite a lot of work to do these days. Have a successful end to the school year and a lovely holiday. Don't forget to let me know what you decide about the cheque for Adèle.

Much love,

Gabrielle

Quebec City, June 21, 1965

Ma chère petite soeur,
I'm enchanted beyond words by your lovely letter, which I've just received, and by your thrilling news and the delight you express for yourself and Clémence[78]. How marvellous it is to be able to make someone happy, or help make someone happy. Would you first of all thank your kind Mother Superior for me, your Mother Provincial,

rather, and the other dear Mother, Luce-Marie. I'm overjoyed at their kindness and consideration for us all. And how can I thank Sister Gilles, who is going to help dear Sister Malvina make Clémence presentable. I know what a thankless chore that's likely to be! A job that will take real Christian love for one's neighbour. My most heartfelt thanks to these two sisters.

I'm sending you $500.00 immediately and please don't stint on anything. This trip must be splendid from beginning to end. I suggest that you take a roomette each so you'll sleep well, or a bedroom for two. You will also need meals on the train, taxis, etc. I wonder if you should stop overnight in Montreal or if you'll be able to make an immediate connection to Quebec City. Then there will be the train from Quebec to Petite-Rivière-Saint-François. Except on Sunday, the daily train leaves Quebec about 2:30 p.m. — there's only one station, the same as for trains from Montreal. If you can arrive in Quebec in time to make this connection, I'd advise you to continue by train all the way to Petite-Rivière-Saint-François, where we'll have been since the first of July. But if you arrive too late for this connection, we'll come and pick you up at the Gare du Palais in Quebec City. You'll have to ask at the Deschambault Agency to get details of the trip and a complete timetable, and let me know in time.

That leaves the question of Adèle. You can hardly go through Montreal without letting her know beforehand, and she'll probably want to see you at least briefly. Of course I'm extending her a sincere invitation to come to Petite-Rivière-Saint-François with the two of you, and I'll pay her travelling expenses as well. If she won't agree to this, perhaps you'd like to stop for a day or two to see her on your way through. Make the suggestion to her, for me, and do whatever you want and feel is best.

Since Clémence must be short of money, give her enough right away, say $100.00 out of the $500.00 I'm sending. If she needs a new suitcase — or anything at all — don't worry about the expense. I don't want you to have to pinch pennies.

Now I must congratulate you heartily for the decision you made about Clémence and the new home[79]. I don't see how you could have done better. I think the change will be good for Clémence. There's just one little worry, I suppose, the fact that she'll be farther away from you and could be lonesome. Still, I imagine that you'll find a way to go and see her from time to time, and that she herself will be able to arrange a ride to town once in a while. In any event, you've done the right thing in the circumstances.

I'm going to telephone right away this evening to rent the little house next door for you. I'm glad you're coming in July because you'll have Marcel's company and he'll be sure to take you on some lovely drives in the car. As for the scenery, I promise you you'll be ecstatic. I can already hear your exclamations of delight. Dear little sister, how happy I am that you've agreed so wholeheartedly to come and see us!

I'll write again soon to let you know what you should bring or not bring. And you'll let me know as soon as your schedule is settled completely and in detail, won't you?

Much love,

Gabrielle

As soon as school is over, start resting as much as you can because the trip will be tiring. I know you, you're going to burn a lot of energy just from enthusiasm, from bubbling over with eagerness and joy. So you'll have to build up a good deal of reserve strength. About Adèle, on second thought perhaps the best thing would be simply to offer her a trip to Manitoba, whenever it suits her. I leave you entirely free to suggest what you think would be best, or even to put off talking to her about it until after you and Clémence have had your own trip. What do you think? Poor thing, I'd like to do something to please her, but everything depends on what mood she's in now, and she certainly mustn't spoil the holiday for the two of you. It's a difficult choice, isn't it? Perhaps the Holy Spirit will guide you in this.

Gabrielle

The postscripts go on and on in this letter. Marcel is delighted over your visit.

P.S. In my excitement I read your letter too quickly, not carefully enough. I've just reread it and see that the answers to all my questions are there. So since you arrive in Quebec City in the evening, we'll come and meet you and take you straight back to Petite-Rivière. The timing will be good since the drive to Petite-Rivière takes a little less than two hours. Everything's settled, then.

Love,

Gabrielle

You could also suggest to Adèle from me — or from you — that if she likes she might travel back with the two of you for a visit to Manitoba, all expenses paid. Do whatever you think is best or even, if you prefer, nothing at all.

Quebec City, June 22, 1965

Ma chère petite soeur,
To follow up the letter I wrote in haste yesterday, here's something I forgot to tell you: if you come all the way to Montreal by CN, you'll probably arrive at Central Station; in that case you'll have to take the train for Quebec from a different station, in other words, go to Windsor Station, which isn't far from Central Station — perhaps a five-minute walk. But since I see that the time between the two trains isn't long, you mustn't dawdle, particularly since it takes a while to get out of Central Station. But there's really no danger of not arriving in time, as long as you pay attention. However, I imagine the Deschambault Agency will make sure you know all you need to know. I slept badly last night, wanting to settle everything in my mind ahead of time. Crazy, isn't it? But we can't change the way we are deep down. I was wondering also if it wouldn't be a good thing to have some mild tranquillizers along during the trip, like Equanil for example, especially for Clémence. If you gave her one an hour before bedtime she'd be sure to have a fairly good night on the train. It would be good for you to take one at bedtime too.

I'm going to have a little bottle of twenty-five tablets sent to you immediately. It's Marcel who suggested it, incidentally. Don't be afraid to take one at night, and have Clémence take one. It's completely harmless and doesn't make you groggy.

Much love,

Gabrielle

Petite-Rivière-Saint-François, July 2, 1965

Chère petite soeur,

I'm writing you in haste about your "petition" on behalf of Sister Henri-de-Marie. I really would like to oblige her and at the same time do you a favour. It won't be easy. Anyway, I don't plan to be in Quebec City between the dates you've given me. It's always difficult to know beforehand when I'm going to be in town — if at all — during the summer. The simplest thing would of course be for Sister Henri to come to Petite-Rivière, but I can't put her up and the village has no hotel facilities. If her cousin could drive her here I could probably give her an hour or two, not really more. Strange as it may seem, it's during the summer holidays that I have most to do. But I think I could give her a little time, particularly in the afternoon, provided she tells me when she's coming at least four or five days before, and at that time gives me an address where I can reach her in case it becomes necessary to call it off; best of all a telephone number where I can leave a message for her.

All things considered, I think the best time for her to come would be while you and Clémence are here, because afterwards I may be going somewhere else for a few weeks. I'm sorry not to be able to do better and hope this will fit in with the time Sister Henri has free.

Rest well. Have you received the Equanil I had the drugstore send you?

A big hug to you till I have the joy of giving you a real one.

Gabrielle

Petite-Rivière-Saint-François [undated, July 1965]

Chère petite soeur,
Yes, of course, you and Clémence will stay here as long as you can. I'm delighted! The little house is ready for you and I think it will be very comfortable. I'm enchanted to be having you for an extra few days, because two weeks really did seem very short for you to see all there is to see and also get some rest.

As for Adèle, I expected that. It's sick, and I'm afraid there's nothing we can do about it. We'll talk about it later. Perhaps she'll accept some money from you when you get back, especially if she's going to be in Manitoba then. And it is true that she lives outside the city so it isn't convenient for her to meet you. Let it go then, and try not to think of it any more, so the holiday will be as happy as possible for you and Clémence.

I've received a letter from Sister Henri about the interview she asked for. Would you be good enough to pass on the arrangements I suggested in my last letter, which will save me having to answer because I don't have much time these days. Tell her I'll see her with pleasure if she can come to Petite-Rivière, but she must try to give me an address or telephone number where I can reach her in case it becomes necessary.

I hope you'll have fine weather for your visit. You're very kind to have paid all those visits. Marcel will be grateful. I expect him any minute because he's been on a little trip for a few days and is due home this evening.

I don't think the Montreal–Quebec train you're going to take has a dining car. It would be a good idea to bring some sandwiches and fruit in case you get hungry. Also, I think it would be best to leave straight from the station for Petite-Rivière as soon as you arrive; that way we won't get home too late, which will be better for all of us. So think of having enough to keep you going until 8:30 or 9:00, the time we'll probably reach home.

Love and kisses,

Gabrielle

Clémence has indeed written me a very sweet letter.

[Undated]

Ma chère Dédette, ma chère Clémence,
Read this note on the train. It will remind you that I'll be with you in my thoughts throughout your trip home, and throughout life. Thank you for coming; I'll see you again many times — probably for ever — in this beloved countryside. Forgive me if I snapped at you a bit at times. It was because of my nerves, you might say, because deep in my heart I was never in the least cross with you. I must be a bit like Papa, poor man, scolding those he loved most. Try not to do too much in Quebec City, so you'll both arrive in Saint-Boniface in good form and still looking healthier than when you came, which I was so happy to see.

Au revoir, my dear little sisters, and may God keep and protect you.

The beautiful river, the gulls, and the mountain will long remember you.

Gabrielle

Petite-Rivière-Saint-François, August 16, 1965

Chère enfant,
We received your two warm and touching letters, one written on the train and the other just after you arrived. Marcel brought me the one you had left in the apartment for me. I've also had a sweet letter from Clémence. So we've been spoiled with these lovely letters; they have gone a long way towards easing my sorrow to see you leave, and some of the loneliness and emptiness I was feeling afterwards. For several days it was as though this beautiful, majestic countryside had nothing left to offer me. I couldn't pass "your" little house, either, without feeling a tug at my heart. Gradually I've become used to the idea that you have both been here and have left again, as if in a dream, yet it was all true. I keep seeing you everywhere: Clémence in the white gloves she wore the first few days, the countless little bouquets of flowers she made, her friend-

ship for the animals. And you, my dear Dédette, the memory of you here, at table, on the porch, in your chair, approaching with your quick little step, none of this is about to fade, I assure you. I was expecting to have a lovely summer with the two of you, but not as lovely as it was, and now looking back it was almost perfect, wasn't it? For if there's nothing under heaven more beautiful than happy, totally successful human relationships, we must agree that they're also the most difficult thing in the world to achieve, and the rarest. But I think we three sisters, with our brother joining in so wholeheartedly, made a kind of small masterpiece of this time together. It has done me a great deal of good too. The pleasure it gave me to see you both so interested in everything and loving everything repaid me far beyond the work it took, which wasn't really tiring because everybody helped.

Marcel left for town yesterday after the weekend and I was supposed to go too, but it was very hot and they were predicting a real heat wave to come, so I decided at the last minute to stay until Wednesday, though I have practically no food left. I'll find a way to manage, however, and I'll be better off here where it's cool.

The neighbours, Jori and Berthe[80], have received your letters and are enchanted with them. Now I must recommend that you slow down your pace and get as much rest as possible, to be in good shape for another year of teaching.

Thank you for the receipt and for running my errands for Léontine.

I hope our kind Sister Gilles will have a speedy recovery. Please give her my warmest regards and all my thanks once again, and my best wishes for her to get well soon.

Oh, how our house, surroundings, and lives needed you, dear little sister, who came out of the sky and left again like a gull! You really did bring this summer a note of poetry and tenderness that we'd never felt before.

All my love,

Gabrielle

I wrote your Mother General the day after you left.

I'll leave it to you to let me know when Clémence needs more money.

G.

Quebec City, October 3, 1965

Ma chère petite soeur,
At last I can send you a set of the photographs taken at Petite-Rivière by our dear neighbour, Berthe. I thought you'd rather have prints than slides, but if you'd like to see the slides too, and if you have a screen and whatever's needed to project them at the convent, I'd be glad to lend you the whole set that I had made for myself. You've no idea how enchanted and moved I was to see these pictures — they've brought the joys of this summer back to life somewhat. I'm particularly fond of the one that shows us at the station, our backs to the paper-brick wall, all three of us a little sad, as though trying to read the future. Who knows, perhaps there are several more happy meetings in store, like this summer's. I don't know if it was as perfect for you as it was for Marcel and me; if so it's almost a miracle. For me, from now on you and Clémence will always in a way be part of the majestic landscape of Petite-Rivière-Saint-François. I can't help seeing and hearing you when I spend a day there.

How is Sister Gilles? Is she better? And how about you? I imagine the trip back must have been fairly taxing. I hear through a letter from Clémence that Adèle came visiting . . . and I gather that perhaps it wasn't all pleasant. Poor you, it makes me sad to think you probably had to listen to complaints. But look at the picturesque Baie-Saint-Paul in the photograph, look at yourself looking at it (how effective that little white winged coif at the edge of the sweeping landscape, and how clever of Berthe to have composed her picture this way); then perhaps your vibrant heart will once again feel a little of the light and joy that bathed the village that day.

Dear little photographs, how I love them for preserving something of this wonderful summer for me!

When you have time, try to let me know how you are — I'm afraid you're terribly tired and can never tell you often enough that you must try to take care of yourself.

A great big hug to you,

Gabrielle

Quebec City, December 3, 1965

Ma chère petite soeur,
I keep remembering the magical times we spent together this summer at Petite-Rivière; they come back to me like pieces of a beautiful dream, and often I still hear you, sitting in your place at my table, exclaiming, "Clémence, is this really us here?" Oh, if only this beautiful thing can happen to us once again in our lives!

If Marcel can find the time, he may go to visit his mother briefly around Christmas, and if he does he certainly won't fail to go and give you a hug. You know he's very fond of you, don't you, you and Clémence? The two of you really entranced him in those weeks you spent with us. You entranced others too, including the Madeleines[81], who often ask after you and call to mind countless recollections of their meeting with "Gabrielle's two sisters". It's because you're both so natural, I think, which makes people feel very close to you the minute they meet you. Incidentally, the Madeleines apologize for not writing to you yet, having been extremely busy, but they said they surely would at Christmastime. And I've also been wanting to tell you that when I appeared briefly at the Salon du Livre, which is held every year in Quebec City, I met Sister Fernand — is that her name? — anyway, your companion when you went with Madeleine Bergeron's chauffeur to see the sights of Quebec City. I thought she seemed perhaps a bit forlorn, alone in the city, and suggested she telephone me, saying that when she did, if I was free at the time, we might meet for an hour of conversation. She hasn't done so yet but I hope she will soon. And your other companion in religious life — I've forgotten her name. Sister Henri, perhaps? The one who is doing a paper on me and who came to Petite-Rivière; was she pleased with her visit? That's a lot of questions, you'll be telling me, and it's not the end of them, because I'm impatient to know if you're well, if you're paying attention to your health, and how you find Clémence. She writes me quite often, the dear thing. In several of her letters I've thought I detected a vague discontent whose source seems to have something to do with Adèle. It's not the first time I've noticed, either, that when Adèle appears Clémence seems depressed. Adèle probably gets her stirred up with her fanciful ideas about them living together. But fortunately in her last letter Clémence seems to have recovered her good humour, so I'm relieved. Besides, I know you won't give in on that point and Clémence will stay where she is. Heaven grant that Adèle too will find some peace and security. Whatever she thinks, there's not a day in my life that I don't wish her this with all my heart. But she won't get there by experimenting with Clémence, far from it. Poor dear you, it's a heavy burden you have on your shoulders, isn't it? I wish it were in my power to relieve you of it.

As for my health, at least that's something you don't have to worry about because on the whole I'm pretty well. My eye is much better because I've been taking big doses of vitamins. That shooting pain there is probably due to chronic neuritis, because the pain goes away with the vitamin treatment. In any event, for the moment it's much better, and in other ways too I'm pretty well.

I imagine you're busy with your birchbark calendars in the little free time you have. I can't look at birch trees any more without thinking of you. I already loved them, so imagine my feeling now when I see them. The most graceful little trees in the world — I say "little" because I'm thinking of our own, which are young trees about fifteen years old now, out on that point where you liked to go and contemplate. Have you ever thought about the way people feel an aura of mystery surrounding things they love? This is a source of constant wonder and delight to me, and must be for you as well.

A big hug to you, hoping there'll be some good news from you very soon. You'll be receiving a box of candies besides the cheque included here, which is meant to help pay your expenses when you're out doing things for Clémence.

With all my love,

Gabrielle

1966 — 1968

Quebec City, January 5, 1966

Ma chère petite soeur,

Your last letter gave me such pleasure, as always; a letter written from the heart and with true affection. Marcel had already told me all about his visits to you and Clémence, but it was good to hear your version. We all have our own version of an event, depending on our way of seeing things, so it's like hearing a different story each time. I'm particularly pleased to know that Clémence has the things she needs, stockings, boots, etc. But Marcel said he thought she was having difficulty reading. Could he be mistaken? She's had new glasses, surely. Poor you, you have to see to so many things. Too many, and I wish I could lighten your burden, because your teaching is already quite enough. I pray God to recompense you with another marvellous trip. You're absolutely right, we must start dreaming of this now. First of all because it can happen and most probably will happen. Maman will see to it from up there in heaven, you can be sure, she so loved to be on the move herself. And then, so that our souls can live and grow they need a dream like this for nourishment. Five years isn't so far off, either.

Clémence wrote a little card, dictated by you, I think, which came yesterday and which we enjoyed very much. The Madeleines have also had a card from her, so everyone is pleased. Surprising as it may seem at first, Clémence really made friends among my friends; they were quite smitten with her and keep asking after her.

As for your little calendars, they're a sensation! Their artlessness, their pleasing colours, the certainty that they're a labour of love, this is why we all love them. Madeleine Bergeron says that hers is the loveliest present she's received this year. And when I look at mine, I see not only a calendar but a little nun in a big apron with a comical straw hat on her head, a slightly mussed little nun with a basin of water at her feet, busy scraping her sheets of birchbark. There aren't many memories as firmly impressed in my mind as this.

When you see that Clémence needs more money, let me know, because she herself rarely tells me of her own accord. It would be wonderful if Adèle returned now to friendship and peace with others. All we can do is pray for her, as you're doing, and I keep hoping, despite all, that this will bring a change of heart in her.

Yesterday the Madeleines and I thought especially of you. We drove up a white, ascending road to a small village in an isolated valley, surrounded by fairly high mountains. There we strapped on our snowshoes and went for a little tour in the brisk but dry and bracing cold. We were talking when we suddenly noticed that the mountain ahead was repeating our words, sending us back a clear, precise echo. Then we amused ourselves royally calling strings of words to this playful mountain and hearing them faithfully repeated. It was an innocent, childlike game, as are the best of games, which is why they do one's heart so much good. And thereupon, my best and most affectionate wishes once again.

Much love,

Gabrielle

Quebec City, April 14, 1966

Ma chère petite soeur,

Your long, lovely letter gave me the greatest pleasure. Apart from the Red River threatening to flood again, all the news it brought was indeed quite good news. Goodness me, I too really wonder where Adèle can have found the money to be going back to Europe. It's true enough that she's trained herself to live on practically nothing all her life, but still!

She must have had some little nest egg put away. Or else someone has left her a small inheritance. She's had some eccentric friends in her time, and perhaps one of them was fairly rich. But what does it matter? I'm happy for her that she's going to have the pleasure of travelling because, when I think of it, travelling seems to have been her real passion in life, the source of her greatest joys.

For Clémence, I enclose a cheque for $100.00. That is, give her some pocket money out of it, say twenty or twenty-five dollars. Then take whatever it's going to cost for glasses and keep the rest in reserve for her. What a business, isn't it, this whole story of the glasses? A real farce. It's a bit like the story of her famous denture in Anna's time, when you and I decided the solution might be to rig Clémence up with a rake instead! You've no idea how many letters we exchanged, just over the denture. A real international incident with hundreds of plots and subplots wouldn't have been more complicated. Anyway, try to settle it once and for all if you can manage, because reading is about the only diversion Clémence has and I'm really anxious for her to be able to do it easily and with pleasure. Otherwise she'll give up reading as well and then, you know, there really won't be much left for her.

I intended to tell you about my trip [to the south of France][82], but there I was started on the subject of the glasses. I think I might spoil it now, no longer being in the mood to begin, so I'll get back to the trip another time. For the moment I'll just say it was mixed, rather like the weather, sometimes exciting, sometimes tiring, on balance very rewarding. I found Paula in great distress, however, having a severe nervous breakdown. It could happen to any of us — no one's immune to this misery. The children are having a terrible time adapting to life in France — it's so strict and demanding after the soft life they led in South Africa. They'll manage it eventually, no doubt, because they're still young, thank God.

The scenery there, like the scenery in Greece, which in fact it resembles, is for my taste the most beautiful and majestic in the world.

I'm delighted you liked the article on me in *Chatelaine*[83] so much. I'm not displeased with it, but I would have liked it better if there had been more to it, more substance and depth.

As for *The Road Past Altamont*[84], which came out a couple of weeks ago, I haven't yet received my copies. As soon as they come I'll send you one. The few people who have read it so far seem to be raving about it. I don't know if that's a good sign. For you anyway, I hope this book brings an especially warm feeling.

Fondest love,

Gabrielle

Yes indeed, how wonderful last summer was for us, and we can see it all the more clearly the farther away it gets, don't you agree?

Petite-Rivière-Saint-François, April 30, 1966

Chère petite soeur,

I've come to spend a while at the cottage, to tidy up a bit and also to get some rest, because my trip to France, for reasons it would take too long to explain, wasn't the easiest I ever took. But never mind, things are better now. I sense you everywhere here, and Clémence as well.

I'm writing you about Clémence, in fact. I've just had a letter from the Minister of National Revenue about the $500.00 income tax exemption they've been giving me for her. They're asking for receipts, but I've never kept track of my expenses on her behalf. Perhaps you could give me a receipt for two or three hundred dollars you've spent for her. Wait until I ask you for it, though, or until the accountant at the firm that looks after my tax declaration asks you for it. It may not be necessary after all. I'm just mentioning it so it won't come as too great a surprise in case someone or other asks you questions about it. Tax investigations over things like this are getting to be tougher.

Don't worry about it, though, because there's really nothing to fear.

I'll write a longer letter soon, and in the meantime my fondest love to you. By the way, the Madeleines were impressed by the tone and polish of the letter you wrote them recently, which they gave me to read and which I too find moving and really beautiful. You write well, Dédette my dear.

My love once again,

Gabrielle

In case the Department of Revenue asks you for receipts or explanations, I enclose a copy of their letter to me and one of my reply.

Quebec City, May 25, 1966

Ma chère petite soeur,

I've been hoping to have a word from you about Clémence's move and what's happening with her plan to go and live with Adèle, but I presume you're very busy and don't have time to do everything, poor child. Or else the news is not very good, as I fear, alas. I would have given anything, and will still give anything, for Clémence to be happy in life — as happy as she can be, and perhaps she hasn't been so happy at Sainte-Anne-des-Chênes[85], but I'm really afraid she's making a change for the worse.

If you see that they need money for some necessity or comfort, like a fridge, etc., I'll send the money to Clémence, so tell me what to do.

For the moment, income tax hasn't asked any more questions about receipts for the small exemption I usually claim for Clémence. Perhaps they'll let it go again this time without too much investigation and bother. If so, you won't have to give me any receipt other than perhaps the usual for a hundred dollars or so for charity, if you can.

I hope with all my heart that living together will work out for Adèle and Clémence, will work out better than I expect, that I'm mistaken about it, because I really am terribly worried. And I'm tired too, for no reason, which will probably pass.

I'm dying to have a letter from you.

Much love,

Gabrielle

Petite-Rivière-Saint-François, June 7, 1966

Ma chère petite soeur,

I received your lovely letter of June 2 and it made me feel very much better. I still have many fears for the future but things are less bleak than I was afraid they'd be, and heavens, perhaps our poor sisters will learn to live together in harmony after all. If that's what happens, I'll be infinitely happy. Do keep me informed of what's going on, and of whatever Clémence may need for one thing or another. Thank you for the receipt. It's a help for my income tax.

About the calendar you sent to Jori, I imagine Mrs. Palmer[86] — who was very pleased with hers, as she has written you, I presume — sent it on to Portugal, where Jori spent the winter. Jori's home now though, and will probably be in Petite-Rivière in a few weeks. I'll ask her then if she did in fact get it. Perhaps Mrs. Palmer kept it for her till she came home. Anyway, don't worry, I'll find out what happened and let you know. One thing I'm sure of, in any event, is that Jori is very fond of you, and she's a person who is very faithful in her friendships and correspondence.

Dear you, I'm so pleased you liked *The Road Past Altamont* so much. I haven't heard anything about the film for a long time[87]. I even thought the whole thing might have gone by the wayside. How did you come to hear of it?

Try to finish up your teaching without getting too tired out. I'm longing for your holidays to come, and for you to have some rest beside your big, beloved lake. You loved it before, but I wonder how you'll think of it now, after reading "The Old Man and the Child" [one of the stories in *The Road Past Altamont*]. I hope your enchantment — great as it was before — will be all the greater.

My love to you, dear little sister. Pray for me.

Gabrielle

How I'd love to think that you were coming again this summer to live in the little house nearby! It speaks to me of you each time I pass. The Madeleines and Berthe send you their best regards. The Madeleines were very touched by the lovely letter you wrote them.

Petite-Rivière, July 28, 1966

Chère petite soeur,
I'm writing you from my swing seat. This summer I can sit outside and swing because the weather has been almost constantly sunny and dry, so there haven't been many of those awful little black flies to plague us as they have in other summers.

All of us hereabouts have received your dear letters. All of us, Jori, Berthe, the Madeleines, and we ourselves, thought they were so like you, vibrant and filled with warmth and gratitude.

I hope your holiday at the lake was as good and enjoyable as ever. You always get so much from it — for body and soul both.

I've written to Clémence since she moved in with Adèle and haven't yet had a reply. Her letter immediately after moving was enthusiastic, which was to be expected, but because she hasn't written a word since I'm rather worried, and have begun to wonder if perhaps she isn't already disappointed. I really hope not, but would you please see her as often as possible and try to gauge the atmosphere between the two of them. It could work, I agree, but I can't help worrying. But you're there to watch out for Clémence, and that's a great comfort in itself.

"Your" little house is rented for the summer to a violinist with the Quebec Symphony Orchestra, a tall, lovely girl, Dutch by origin, who comes with her dog for three days every week, to practise the violin. It's delightful. On the other hand, Jori has rented a country house near Montreal and will probably sell this one if she can find a buyer, which isn't easy around here. She spent a good part of July at Petite-Rivière, in very good form, in better health than ever, in fact. When she speaks of you, it's always most warmly. The Madeleines are spending the summer twenty miles from here, at Les Eboulements, where, if you remember, you take the ferry for Ile-aux-Coudres. Their friend Jean Palmer bought an enchanting little Quebec-style house there — a bit like the one you and Clémence were in — and has rented it to the Madeleines for the season. But I've no doubt they'll write you and tell you all about it, and I don't want to deprive them of their pleasure.

Altogether, the weather has been splendid. So we've been able to get a lot of sunshine, which has been good for me.

I hope this lovely summer is being and will continue to be good to you also. My love to you. If anything's amiss with Clémence, let me know without delay.

Love and kisses,

Gabrielle

Marcel thanks you for your sweet letter and sends you his affectionate regards.

Quebec City, January 25, 1967

Chère petite soeur,
Forgive me, in my last two letters I forgot to thank you for the lovely mitts for taking hot dishes from the oven. They'll be very useful, because I often burn my hands when I do a bit of cooking.

I also meant to thank you for the association's[88] anniversary programs. I have the impression that your theatrical sketches must have been as great a success as always, buoyed by all that enthusiasm of yours, like a lighthearted breeze.

The text I wrote for Expo '67 on the theme "Man and His World" will be made into an Expo souvenir album with pictures and a preface, probably by Monsieur Dupuis, Commissioner General of Expo, and will be sold to the public[89]. If you aren't in too much of a hurry to read it, I'd almost rather you waited until I send you an album. Anyway, for the moment I don't have a copy available. I hope with all my heart that the changes that may be made to some of the rules and customs of your community won't be too drastic, and that you'll be able to adapt to those that are inevitable without too much difficulty. Perhaps you shouldn't get too upset about them. As long as one's heart is free, what do life's little necessities matter?

I'd like to see you less busy, however. Short of giving up teaching altogether, couldn't you teach just a few hours a day?

You were probably right to buy a small radio for Clémence,

although she has plenty of money for those things; you could have kept what it cost for your shopping, etc. I'll write again soon.

Much love,

Gabrielle

Quebec City, April 5, 1967

Ma chère petite soeur,
Your lovely letter just arrived and I'm answering right away because I'm fairly free at the moment and may as well take advantage of it. I'm glad you were able to have those few days of rest at Saint-Pierre, and very glad, yes, very glad indeed to hear that you'll only have half a day of teaching next year. I think it's quite enough for someone who's done as much as you, when you haven't ever had a strong constitution. And then I think it's best to give up a little at a time and not too suddenly. All these changes you tell me about are hard to accept when you've reached a certain age and aren't as adaptable as you once were. I think also that the times we're living in now are caught up in a frenzy of change, some of which is good, but not all. Really, humans are a great flock of sheep, or at least behave like sheep, all turning together this way or that without knowing where it's taking them, but I think we must have confidence in the ultimate end of all this prodigious human effort. This is what I was trying to say in my article for the Expo book[90].

I'm sending Clémence a bottle of vitamins without delay and I've dropped her a line to tell her about the lovely visit we had at Yolande's during the Easter holiday[91]. All of them, she, Jean, and the children, were charming, amusing, and delightful. The baby is lively and cheerful. Gisèle is becoming a little person who thinks and reflects about everything, and she's ravishingly beautiful with those huge, often dreamy eyes of hers.

Now that Clémence has her full pension, I won't be able to get any tax deduction at all for her. I could claim charitable deductions, however, so could you get me a receipt for $100.00? You could keep part of this sum for yourself, taxi fare etc., and with the rest see to buying whatever Clémence may need as the year goes on. Or just set it aside for unforeseen difficulties or circumstances. I sometimes tell myself that perhaps we'll be lucky enough to have another get-together at Petite-Rivière or Quebec before many more years go by. Perhaps we'll be granted this happiness one more time, I say to myself. So it would be wise to put a little money aside with this in mind.

Thank you for your sweet letter. Marcel sends you his best regards. We both think of you with much affection. The enchanting memory you left at Petite-Rivière is not about to fade away, do please believe this. Everyone there still loves the "little sister", as they call you.

My fondest love to you,

Gabrielle

How about you, do you think we can get together once more by the sea and in the peace and quiet of the country?

Petite-Rivière-Saint-François, June 6, 1967

Ma chère petite soeur,
I've just arrived here for the summer, or part of the summer, and must write you at once; for me Petite-Rivière is still so filled with incomparable memories of the summer you were here with Clémence. It never fails: whenever I pass the little house you lived in, I see your two faces and hear your voices. If only it could all happen at least once more; this is my fervent hope. The weather is beautiful, very warm the last while for this time of year. Today it's raining, and this is good, because there was a danger of drought. Marcel will be happy for his flower garden, which is well under way. Jori should arrive soon to spend a month, I think, in her house. Berthe Simard often mentions your visit and speaks of you with deep affection. We're making plans for the day when it may be possible to have you come again.

Have you received my cheque? Could you send me a receipt for income tax deduction? There's no hurry, of course. I only want to be sure you did get the money. For a long letter from you, I know I'll probably have to wait until holiday time at the lake. And I don't doubt that you'll once again write me a long, wonderful letter, the one I think of as "the summer letter", or "Dédette's hymn to creation". As for me, I'll surely write you again before long. I also plan to write Clémence very soon.

Much love,

Gabrielle

Quebec City, October 18, 1967

Ma chère petite soeur,

Just a line that I've snatched time for, to thank you for your sweet letter and try to cheer you up a bit, for alas, what else can I do for the moment? I was terribly distressed to hear the latest about Clémence's move. It's plain to see that poor Adèle has fouled things up again, really wrecked things. I've spent hours trying to think of a solution, and I don't see one. For the moment, what can we do except pray that things will change for Clémence? She'll surely begin to waste away from nervous prostration again if we don't get her out of there soon. I think what makes her ill and listless is a lack of air more than anything else. I know too well Adèle's habit of blocking the least crack through which a little fresh air might enter. In summer, when Clémence could get outside every day, she could at least get rid of the poisons. But now . . . !

Oh, my dear little sister, how heavy my heart is to see you coping all alone with these problems and to feel so powerless to ease Clémence's predicament. She asked for it, of course, but that doesn't change the fact that she's miserable now. Go this instant and ask the good Lord to help us make sure Clémence has a better roof over her head.

I'll write again soon.

Love,

Gabrielle

Quebec City, November 29, 1967

Ma chère petite soeur,
At last I've heard from Clémence that she's given up living with Adèle and gone back to The Presentation[92]. It may not be ideal but I imagine you feel, as I do, that it's infinitely better for Clémence than life with poor Adèle. Anyway, I was very relieved to hear the news and can guess that you had to work hard to bring it about. I'm glad for Clémence, and also for Adèle, really. Thank you, little sister.

Pauline Boutal[93] was in Quebec City briefly, and though she didn't have time to come and see me she telephoned and we had a long talk, largely about you. As I listened I had the pleasure of realizing once again how much she likes and admires you. You have a friend there who's very, very fond of you.

Marcel and I are just back from a short trip to Ottawa. We were there for the Order of Canada investiture ceremony, as guests of the government[94]. I received a medal along with thirty-four fellow Companions and about fifty other people. It's a magnificent medal, enamel with a gold border, a six-pointed design representing the six points that snowflakes always have, whatever their form, which varies infinitely. The obverse bears the Canadian symbol, our maple leaf, and the reverse the word *Canada* and a number, 42 in my case, meaning that I'm the forty-second in the order. So there's no name, which I find more dignified. As for the motto, which is struck in small letters around the maple leaf on the obverse, it's very fitting, even inspired, I think, in these troubled times. Translated from the Latin, it means *desirers of a better country.* How better could it be said, don't you agree?

I don't know what to tell you about the ceremony, except that it was very simple and full of dignity, warmth, and grace. I don't think I've ever in my life seen anything of this kind more effective, more imposing, yet less pretentious. At the end, when we stood up, the whole audience and the Companions, both French- and English-speaking, to sing "O Canada", the depth of emotion we all felt was clear to everyone, I think. I had imagined that such a beautiful ceremony would be televised from beginning to end, and most of it was in fact filmed, but practically nothing was shown to the public. Either it's being kept for later or, as I alas fear, those beautiful scenes of union were discarded to make room for films showing the sessions of the Etats-Généraux, which were taking place the same evening and which seemed much more committed to separating Canadians[95]. What difficult times we're living through now in Quebec! On all sides tempers are frayed, and emotions are intense. Soon, I suppose, we're going to have to take sides against each other. There's already practically an atmosphere of revolution. And that great duffer de Gaulle had to go and stick his nose in our business again![96] As you can see, my emotions are very mixed these days. Yours too, of course, because everything has begun to change so quickly. Perhaps it's a sign that humanity is evolving faster. But it's getting so difficult to follow, to adapt.

I'm going to send you some candies for Christmas. I'll send some to Clémence too. In this letter, please find a cheque for $125.00. I thought you could give $25.00 to Clémence from me now for pocket money, keep $25.00 as a present for yourself, and put the rest away to be spent later, some for you and some for Clémence, as you think best. I've just had a good supply of vitamins sent to her, however, so she won't need any more of those for a while.

Could you send me a receipt for this $125.00 as a charitable donation, deductible for my income tax? I'd like you to date it January 1968, the 2nd or 3rd, whichever you like.

Dear little sister, how happy I would be to see you again! Marcel may perhaps go and see his mother at Christmas, and if he does he'll be sure to go and give you a hug from me.

As for me, I'm feeling a great urge to go south this winter, to store up some sunshine and warmth. I'll talk to you about this later, if I get around to making a decision.

My fondest love and most affectionate and heartfelt wishes,

Gabrielle

In Ottawa we spent a whole day with Yolande, Jean, and the children, who were adorable.

P.S. Having just finished my letter, I received yours with all the details about settling Clémence, so I'm reassured and enormously pleased. So things are going a good deal better on that score. Mostly thanks to you. Heaven be praised!

Try now to be careful and not get too tired.

Gabrielle

Do you ever hear from Paul Painchaud and Fernand and Léontine?

New Smyrna Beach [Florida], February 19, 1968

Ma chère petite soeur,
Did you get the photograph of me at the Order of Canada investiture, which I sent before leaving for Florida? My wonderful stay here is nearly over — well, not quite, since I'm not going home until March 15. In a way I've liked it here as much as at Petite-Rivière. And I think it's done me even more good, because there's plenty of sunshine and although by the sea it's not damp, thanks to a constant breeze on the beach. I've been almost completely free of sneezing and also the pain in my eye. My sleep has improved too. I've also met some very fine Canadians here, among them — strange, isn't it? — Hector Allard[97], who's now retired, with his wife Marie-Nicole, a Frenchwoman, whom I find amusing, clever, and very engaging. We see each other quite often. The rest of the time I like to go for walks alone on the endless stretch of beach that's as white as a snow-covered plain, and along the waterline dotted with terns, gulls, and *maubèches*, little birds with long skinny legs that keep running down to meet a wave, and then back up to escape it. Have you ever seen them on your beloved Lake Winnipeg? "Our" beloved Lake Winnipeg! In English they're called "sandpipers", I think.

I also went with some friends on a short car trip inland where they grow oranges in huge orchards and, farther south, vegetables as far as you can see. Florida is a very beautiful place and I'd very much like to be one of those people who have a house here for the winter. We'll see about this later, perhaps.

How are you, dear child? And Clémence? And Adèle? I enjoyed your story of the birthday party for three given at Sainte-Anne-des-Chênes.

Much love,

Gabrielle

[Postcard from Florida, undated]

Chère petite soeur,
The climate here is doing me a lot of good. I'm right beside one of the most beautiful beaches I've ever seen — fine, white, firm sand you can walk on without getting tired, to the sound of crashing waves and the dear little cries of terns — not sad like gulls' cries. I haven't felt so much at ease in a place for a long time. Will you join me in my prayer of thanks? I'll be here for another month. I have some delightful friends in the town. Thank you for your sweet letter and the lovely apron you sent at Christmas. Also for the charity receipt.

Love,

Gabrielle

[Undated, postmarked February 26, 1968]

New Smyrna is very old. Shortly after the voyage of Ponce de Léon, a Spanish explorer of these shores, New Smyrna was founded with the help of a handful of Greeks, Minorcans, and Italians. The wife of the founder, whose name was Turnbull, was Greek, born in Smyrna in Asia Minor. This is how the place came by its name, in honour of the founder's Greek wife. There are a good many historic sites of very great interest here, and also more or less all along the coast, where the Spanish and French, mostly the Spanish, left vestiges of their presence, which was often cruel and tumultuous.

It's been cold, even in Florida, cold enough to freeze in some places. But today they're predicting 68 — which probably means 70 or more in the sun. I'm hoping it will be warm for my last two weeks.

I have a seashell for you that I'm going to keep until I can send it to you, or — who knows? — put it in your hand myself.

Love,

Gabrielle

Petite-Rivière-Saint-François, July 3, 1968

Ma chère petite soeur,
I received your letter yesterday and hasten to reply. We'll have to hope that Clémence can get into Otterburne[98], because being bounced around as she is with Adèle is just too awful and too depressing. Oh, why couldn't Adèle have left her at Sainte-Anne[99] where she was all right, and where she might still be doing quite well if she'd stayed? How thoughtless of Adèle to play with a human life like that! Do all you can, then, to find a suitable place for Clémence, and let's both pray that you'll succeed. I'd really like to come to Manitoba to give you a hand, but I don't know anyone there any more and I'd feel such a stranger, so could I even do as well as you? Besides, where would I stay? Léa's so good[100] she'd take me in, there's no doubt, she's told me so time and again, but if I stayed with her (Léa) my mother-in-law would raise the roof and there'd be no end to the scolding I'd get. And going to stay with her is something I just can't face. Of course, if you really need me I'll come and put up with all the awful trouble I foresee — certainly the possibility of having to see Adèle; who knows how she'll behave with me? Perhaps not so badly after all. Anyway, that's not what really puts me off coming; as I've said, it's Marcel's mother, who's impossible to get along with. Dear child, let's hope you find a good niche for Clémence, as you've done in the past. Anything will be better for her than living with Adèle, won't it? Poor dear you, you really are burdened with a lot of cares, troubles, and responsibilities. Have you considered how strange it is, when you've chosen a life that's at least removed from this kind of responsibility, if not really insulated from it, that so much responsibility has fallen on you? Bless you for what you're doing. I've often called on Maman for help, and now let's both pray that she'll come to your aid and inspire and guide you well.

So I'll wait to hear from you again, here at Petite-Rivière. Don't hesitate to tell me if you need more money. In case you need to reach me quickly, I'm giving you my telephone number at the cottage — the telephone was put in a year ago — an unlisted number; write it down where you won't risk losing it. You can call me collect.

You can be sure I'll agree with whatever you decide for Clémence, after you've consulted her doctor and, I'm sure, several of your companions who have good judgement.

Tell poor Clémence that I think of her all the time and, to encourage her, that I may try to come and see her before long. And to see you too, my dear Dédette; what a joy and comfort that would be! Now that I'm back at Petite-Rivière, you've no idea how often I think of your visit three years ago. I see you everywhere and my heart aches. I bless heaven that we had this marvellous time together, but I really would like to have another. We've seen so little of each other all our lives.

I hope with all my heart that your health will withstand all the strain, and that you'll have a good holiday. You need it badly.

My fondest love,

Gabrielle

Petite-Rivière-Saint-François, August 25, 1968

Ma chère petite soeur,
I've received your lovely letter, which Marcel brought me on the weekend, and hasten to thank you for all your efforts on behalf of Clémence. Since I don't have her new address, I'm sending her a letter through you. You may read it of course, which will save me repeating myself and saying all over again what I've already told her. You'll see that I've been at Petite-Rivière for ages, which I'm far from sorry about, but I've been terribly lonely at times. Alone with the sea, one is bound to have moments of misery. But also inexpressibly wonderful moments.

I would really have liked to go and see you in Manitoba, but all in all I think it's better to put off getting together until a day soon when, I hope, it can happen in better circumstances. At least in peace and harmony if possible.

Jori has also spent the whole summer here, in her house across the road, and has been painting portraits of children this year — very beautiful, very successful. She's in better health, is in high spirits, and gives delightful little parties every so often for her friends from Baie-Saint-Paul and Les Eboulements, which is to say, city people on holiday. For me it's an opportunity to meet her painter and artist friends, who are all outstanding and engaging people. The painter Jean-Paul Lemieux comes, and sometimes comes to my house too. He and his wife keep asking after you. So does Jori, often, having the warmest and most cordial and affectionate memories of you. Everyone hopes to see you again one day.

Are you going to teach again this year? Part of the day? What subjects? I hope you can turn down anything too heavy and can arrange to get enough rest. You with your "gung-ho" nature, I'm always afraid you'll get overtired.

I'd be grateful if you could keep giving me fairly frequent news of Clémence, if only a few quick lines. As for Otterburne, we'll have to be prepared to have patience, because Clémence certainly won't get a place until one comes free. Life is cruel in a way, because what we're really doing is hoping for someone to pass away to make room for Clémence.

I'm confident it will happen. What frightens me is that if the wait is too long, Clémence will slip back into a state of apathy and hopelessness.

Pray for us all, dear, kind little sister, and take care of yourself for my sake.

Fondest love,

Gabrielle

Thank you for your news of Léa. I'll write her soon. Thank you too for your visit to our dear Antonia.

Quebec City, October 16, 1968

Ma chère petite soeur,
Today I'm having a copy of the complete "Le Thème raconté" sent to you — that's the text I wrote for the *Man and His World* book[101]. You must be sure to return this to me after having some copies made, because

it's the only one I have of the full text. Tell Sister Rachel that I wish her all the luck in the world.

It's strange [what you say] about Clémence because I'd just been writing to her. In her last letter Léa had in fact told me that Clémence was much better. It's almost a miracle, and something to rejoice over. If she goes to Aunt Anna's she must be careful of the food there, because much of it will be too greasy for her. As for Adèle, of course I have no intention of harming her. I've never harmed her and will never try to. It's all in her mind. What hurts me terribly is that she's been introducing herself everywhere as my sister and then proceeding to malign me. It's happened at the Montreal Municipal Library and elsewhere. The saddest part is that she doesn't even serve her own cause when she behaves this way, because it creates a bad impression. Many similar stories have come to my ears indirectly, so I can imagine she's been finding fault with me to a lot of people in a lot of places. I've been told something else, too: that she thrusts her work on people, so to speak, then if they turn it down she insults them or writes rude letters.

Perhaps she'll have some success this time; I hope so with all my heart. I'll be the first to be happy if the enormous amount of work she's done finally brings her some satisfaction and reward. But she'll have to learn that she can't impose herself — only the quality of the work should count — and that it does her no good to use my name, particularly if she goes on to cast all those slurs at me. A good deal of this sort of thing has come back to me — I hate to have to say it — which is embarrassing and hurts me deeply.

Be that as it may, if she gets in touch when she's in Quebec City I'll treat her as nicely as I can, that goes without saying, but I very much doubt she will.

All this is so painful it's hard to bear, God knows, and I can do nothing about it.

About the copy I'm sending you — it isn't great either, I see. I don't have the original, having sent it to a "high-placed person" who never returned it. But Sister Rachel may perhaps get better results with this one anyway.

Affectionately,

Gabrielle

Quebec City, October 18, 1968

Ma chère petite soeur,
A line to follow up my letter of a few days ago. I've just heard that two or three years ago Adèle was submitting a manuscript to almost all the publishers in Montreal, and elsewhere too (even one in Worcester in the United States), in which she told the story, her own spiteful version, of my childhood, my life. Were you aware of anything so abominable? Some of my friends were, but hid it from me out of kindness. The other evening I was at the house of some friends when the cat was finally let out of the bag and I learned the whole mortifying story. Someone there had seen the manuscript but didn't want to say much about it, except, of course, that it was intended to hurt me, and was as unkind as could be. True, no one would publish this text, but it was going the rounds from one publisher to another for a long time, and if it had fallen into the hands of someone who wished me harm it could have been used against me. I didn't tell you this story at first, for fear it would upset you as deeply as it has me. Everyone agrees that something like this is the work of a sick person. In fact, I've thought for quite some time that Adèle might be a lot sicker than Clémence. Finally I decided I'd have to let you know, in case you have enough influence with her to get her to stop behaving this way, if at all possible, though I'm afraid she's beyond reasoning with.

She must have been thinking of writing something to hurt me for a long time, because Anna suspected as much and warned me[102]. I think she would have thought twice about trying to sell such a text to the public when Anna was alive, though. Anyway, this manuscript is surely still in existence; it's a kind of threat to me, to us all, and I suspect Adèle of doing everything possible to have it made public some day, even after her death. I realize now that her hatred of me is implacable, close to lunatic. If ever you can get your hands on that text and destroy it, you'll do everyone a great service, and harm no one.

So this is a gloomy letter, my dear little sister. It hurts me to have to write it, and to think that you'll have to read it. I hope I'll never have to mention the subject again. Perhaps God will inspire you with some way of bringing Adèle to destroy such evil writings herself. Or some other way of handling it. Anyway, your prayers alone will be a great help to me. I'm not telling Marcel about any of this, of course, I'm so humiliated by it all.

Affectionately,

Gabrielle

I hope to write you a more cheerful letter next time.

Quebec City, October 30, 1968

Ma chère petite soeur,
I've just received your letter and hasten to reassure you. Don't worry too much over the business I was telling you about. You know about it, that's the most important thing. Don't do anything for the moment; don't even write to Adèle. It's best not to let her have possession of anything written, except things that are totally innocuous. Just keep your eyes open, that's all. If the opportunity arises, tell her to her face whatever you think you ought to say, but don't give her any weapons to use against either you or me. With her, I'm afraid that's always a danger. Just pray, this is the best thing you can do for the moment, I think.

Besides, poor Adèle's manuscripts aren't as dangerous as one might suppose; they lack as much in interest as in other ways, simply because she's so totally absorbed with herself. Anyway, so far, according to what I've been told, all the publishers who have seen this supposed story of my life have turned it down flat.

So don't be too upset. When I learned how far she had carried things, I jumped out of my skin and had to tell you. Now I'm a bit less worried, and perhaps it's because of your prayers.

Dear child, I'm sorry I had to trouble you. Perhaps you'll have an opportunity to touch a chord in Adèle's heart one day, though I'm not so sure, I doubt it, but who knows? In order for her to feel differently towards me I'd have to give her something that's not in my power to give — the gift of really being able to capture the interest of others. And how could she have it, the poor sick thing, living such a totally self-centred existence?

As you've seen yourself, she constantly absolves herself and lays blame on others. So it is with Sister C. So it is with all such people, really.

So just observe and say nothing for the moment, stop worrying, and don't make a move till the time is ripe, if it ever is; I don't think it's ripe now.

Ever so much love,

Gabrielle

I've had a sweet letter from Clémence, who at least seems to be better, so there's something to cheer us, isn't there?

Whatever you do, don't let Adèle know you learned all this from me. She'll deduce that we're plotting against her and will be all the more determined to hurt me. Don't forget to return my copy of "Le Thème raconté", though there's no hurry.

Quebec City, November 15, 1968

Ma chère petite soeur,
I had a lovely visit from Yolande and Jean recently. It will be their last before they leave for France at the beginning of December. They're as happy as can be with what's happening to them, and I think they're the right age to get the most out of a spell in Europe. I find them more discerning and cultivated every time I see them, too. They told me that Adèle had spent three days with them, was apparently delighted to be so nicely treated, and was in pretty good humour, except of course that she was finding fault with everyone, as usual. Yolande thinks she remembers grasping from the flood of words, which she was only half

listening to, that Adèle was coming to Quebec City to deposit some important papers in the Archives. This could well be the manuscript I told you about, of whose existence I have no proof except that good friends have told me they've seen it with their own eyes. Adèle could also be coming to deposit personal letters in the Archives. Or it's possible that she's just coming to look for information. Whatever it is, there's nothing to be done except pray, because I'm afraid that trying to make her listen to reason — did we ever succeed? — would only make things worse. So for the moment just drop the whole thing, unless an opportunity suddenly arises for you to step in, which I doubt. According to what Yolande tells me, Adèle has it in for you too, poor child, for having entered religious life so young — imagine!

Now, that's enough about that! I hope we won't have to talk about it any more. Since I have so much trouble with my sinusitis, sore throats, and headaches as soon as the cold sets in, I'm going to leave a bit earlier for Florida. I'll probably leave on December 12. I'm enclosing the two addresses where you can reach me; I'll be at the first until January 1st, beginning December 12, and the second for the rest of my stay. It keeps my spirits up to think of the peacefulness and beauty I'm going to find there again, and of the good the sea air does me. Later I'll tell you more about this corner of the world that I'm so fond of. Before leaving, I'll send you a little cheque as a Christmas present. (On second thought, I'd better send it now.)

Try to spare your strength, dear child, and keep yourself in as good health as possible. I'm praying for you with all my heart and hope you're doing the same for me.

Much love,

Gabrielle

Spend this little bit of money on yourself, on some little treat or other small thing you might like.

As I was about to seal my letter, yours arrived, a very heartwarming letter. I'm glad about Clémence, she'll surely be better there. However, we'll have to expect her to be lonely so far away from you and Saint-Boniface. To the extent that it's possible, do try to go and see her often. So you can do so, I'll send you a large cheque early in 1969, for which you can send me a receipt for charity, and the money will be put to the best use in the world, it seems to me, if it allows you to go and spend a day with Clémence or take her out once in a while.

Yes, I've often thought about going back to Phoenix, where I loved the scenery and climate. At New Smyrna, though, I've found an efficiency that's very pleasant and doesn't cost too much, and I have some friends there. For this winter anyway, I'm planning to go there. Not without some regret, because I'm fond of Fernand and Léontine. A pity that Florida and Arizona are so far apart, because otherwise I could have done both. About the manuscript Adèle has put into the hands of Monseigneur G., I hope he does take an interest in it. What I've heard — not in this case especially but in general — is that people don't dare turn down a manuscript of Adèle's in her presence, she's so insistent, threatening even, but behind her back they say loudly and clearly what they think. If she could have some success, her life and state of mind would both certainly be pleasanter, which is what I've always most sincerely wished for her, whatever she thinks. But I can't twist people's arms to make them be interested in the things she writes.

My love to you again, dear little sister, and thank you warmly for the care you're giving Clémence.

Gabrielle

Marcel was rather overworked and tired during the summer, but he's been quite a bit better the last while. He's a bundle of nerves and doesn't know how to relax. Otherwise he's well. You may see him if he decides to take his little trip to Manitoba for Christmas.

1969

New Smyrna Beach, January 22, 1969

Ma chère petite soeur,

I'm devastated to hear that you no longer have your diction class . . . really, really devastated. It's a cruel age in every way for anyone who's getting on in years. . . . Before you can turn around, you're on the shelf. I know something about this, you know, for all the honours, which are like a kind of burial rite, in fact — rather depressing when they coincide with fewer readers and fewer sales . . . a decline of a sort. . . . But I'm not writing you just to complain, which is something we should probably never do; an unhappy letter is so hard on the person receiving it.

I want to thank you for your kind prayers — the best of anything you could do for me. Also for your advice, which is well meant; only it doesn't do any good, you know, to say, "Compare, see what your life is like compared to this one's or that one's" — because you never know everything you need in order to make a judgement; you only have appearances, and appearances are not always the truth. A person who appears to have everything, as they say, may be torn apart beyond all imagining, while another whose life looks very difficult may not be as unfortunate as you might think. But I know you're doing your best to be helpful, and I'm grateful and I too will pray for you; you never complain, though you're not immune either to trials and sorrows. And now that's enough of such things; let's try a more cheerful subject. I'm pleased to see how well you and Adèle are looking after Clémence. In a way she's the one in the family who's the best cared for, as it turns out, and I praise heaven for it.

The weather has been glorious here for the past three or four days, lovely summery days freshened by a warm, slightly moist breeze. And always the everlasting murmur of the sea. Lord, what a mysterious thing is our existence, so grand in some ways, in others so wretched.

I'm pleased that Sister Rachel-Eveline should write about my essay on *Man and His World*, at which I worked so hard and which has not had nearly the exposure it deserved, perhaps. It was an ill-fated effort, and the grief it cost me is all the greater now in retrospect, to think that it might have inspired a great many people — at least, this is the way I see it when I'm not not feeling too low. Anyway, it's good of Sister Rachel to bring out the theme of the piece, which I believe in passionately.

Keep praying for me, dear little sister, and give Clémence my affectionate wishes.

Much love,

Gabrielle

New Smyrna Beach, February 25, 1969

Ma chère petite soeur,

Thank you for your delightful letter, so full of affection and interesting news. E.K. should have written to say that she'd received the copy of the *Man and His World* text, but she is an extraordinarily busy woman and is never still, travelling back and forth between Carleton where she teaches and Montreal where she tapes her lectures, when she isn't somewhere else interviewing someone. How nice that her lectures interest young people. I'm very pleased. I'm even more pleased that you've found Clémence to be in fairly good shape. Just before your letter came I'd received a rather doleful one from her. "It's boring. . . . It isn't Saint-Boniface. . . . This place is way out in the country. . . . It's really the wilderness. . . ." I think she's got into the habit of picking on anything at all to complain about. In any event, she couldn't be better off anywhere else than she is there, don't you agree?

I'm enclosing a cheque for $125.00 to be used however you think best — for you, for her, or for trips from Saint-Boniface to Otterburne[103]. As soon as you get it, would you be good enough to send me a receipt for my income tax? It's not yet certain that Marcel will come [to Florida], and if he does it will only be for eight or nine days. It's a shame because I'm convinced that a fairly long stay would settle his nerves and greatly improve his state of health. I arrived here myself in a terrible state, and now I'm a thousand times better. On the other hand I haven't been sleeping very well, though I'm afraid this runs in the family.

I've often wondered if there might be a small chance of being able to bring you here, perhaps with Clémence, for three or four weeks. But I know it's pure fantasy. As for this summer, my poor child, I'm still quite unable to make a decision, owing to a climate of uncertainty and a lot of other reasons. Perhaps God will arrange a meeting for us at another time. Keep praying for me. I'm convinced your loving thoughts and prayers create a kind of protective ambience around me and sustain me.

Much love,

Gabrielle

New Smyrna Beach, March 8, 1969

Ma chère petite soeur,

Thank you for your sweet letter and the receipt. As for the trip that you and Clémence want so much to make this summer to visit me, I've been thinking about it almost constantly since you first mentioned it, believe me, but for the moment I still can't make any decision. I don't want to dampen all hopes of it for you, or create false ones. I'm going to do everything I can, though I can't be sure it will work out, because there are a lot of difficulties. A place to stay to begin with, because Berthe no longer has her little house for rent, and she doesn't want to rent rooms in her big house because she's keeping them for her own visitors, who come constantly. Supposing I do find a way to have you come, I don't know when it will be, in July or not till August. It depends on Marcel's holidays and other things I have to take into account. In any event, at best I don't think I can give you an answer before, say, the end of May, which is late for your preparations, but I really can't do any better. First of all I'll have to see if Marcel is better, what his plans are, a whole lot of things, and I'm most terribly sorry, I assure you, not to seem more enthusiastic. If the trip can't be arranged for this summer you might ask for some kind of travel permission in advance, explaining that it might have to be postponed till later or cancelled. And instead of the trip to Quebec, if it's possible you might take Clémence for a couple of weeks to some restful place, Kenora, for example. Anyway, I don't want you to have too high hopes, so you won't be too disappointed if our plans don't come to anything.

What we'd have to find would be a little house to rent that's fairly close to mine, where, if need be, you could have your first two meals of the day. You would have supper quietly at my house. This is a plan that occurs to me, only I don't know of a house, except too far away in the village. Supposing I do find one, you'd have to be ready to take it when it's available, and when Marcel and I are there as well. That's a lot of "ifs".

In any event, I'll see if it can be done as soon as I'm home and can go to Petite-Rivière.

Goodness knows, I too will be glad for Adèle if she makes good, if her book's a success[104]. I'd like nothing better, but a book is liked or not liked on its own merits. I hope with all my heart that she'll be rewarded for all her work and perseverance. I just wonder if there's a big enough readership for books like hers, especially these days when really good books are difficult to sell, unless they're out to make a sensation.

Do you think Clémence is well enough to make the long trip east? Personally, I confess I'm worried. Most of all because we'll have to watch her to make sure she doesn't go off her diet, and prepare meals that observe the diet, and take into account her having no teeth. Oh my, the complications! When it comes to adventurousness, Mother Mélina's daughters run true to form.

I'll be back in Quebec City around the 26th or 28th very probably.
My fondest love,

Gabrielle

I told Madame K. I'd be back later to save myself from her invitation to be interviewed, certainly a well-intentioned invitation, but my nerves are still too frayed and fragile for this kind of ordeal on television, which is very hard to take, believe me.

Don't, I beg you, go and promise anyone, whoever it is, that you'll intercede with me to obtain an interview or anything else, because I hate refusing, you know, and if I do it's because my health or other pressing reasons oblige me to.

G.

New Smyrna Beach, March 15, 1969

Ma chère Bernadette,
This is the way you signed your precious birthday card, and it's strange how this simple thing reached my heart, quite bowled me over[105]. I've just now received the card, present, and letter — the letter so moving and tender that I'm still all upside down inside. I've often had the feeling that your affection for me — for all of us in the family — has been growing, radiating more and more warmly as the years have passed. This time, however, you've understood my dilemma so well, sensed all the difficulties I'm coping with so accurately, that I'm both relieved and saddened. You're right, let's wait for a sign showing us a little more clearly that the time has come for the two dear souls in Manitoba to set out for the East. But I do hope this sign will come soon, because I too want it to happen, perhaps as much as you and poor dear Clémence. For the moment, it really is difficult for me to plan much ahead, even a few months. Still, I don't know why but I'm confident our wish will come

true when the right time comes. Keep praying for me, for Marcel, and for the happiness we'll have when we're all together. The opportunity may arise, the way may open unexpectedly.

I've already read a chapter of the book you so kindly sent me. I was attracted immediately by its sincerity, its honesty, then suddenly saw that I agreed with the author's approach. You can be sure that I'll read it carefully, and I think it will enlighten and cheer me. Thank you, Dédette mine. Still, what has gladdened my heart most of all is your letter, you know. When I see you so goodheartedly give up a plan so dear to you, I also see it as an eloquent sign of your deep and genuine affection for me. But may God still grant us our wish.

A big, warm hug to you. Do try to give Clémence the same kind of confidence and hope you've transmitted to me. Where would we be without you? Now I'm anxious to get back to Quebec City. By and large my stay in Florida has been good for me, although I didn't succeed in doing any work. I just couldn't. There has been a total void in my head. At times I've been very depressed. Yet I do think my health has improved and as to the rest, who knows, perhaps I'll realize later that it's been good for me in another way as well, as an after-effect. Sometimes we take a while to appreciate the benefit of certain things that happen to us. As I wrote in *Street of Riches*, "our joys take time to catch up with us". I've had a line from Madame K., who was immensely pleased with your letter. She worries about not understanding the underlying meaning and symbolism in my books, and you've reassured her.

A hug to you once again. I'd love to have another letter from you soon.

Gabrielle

You must admit there's some good in the changes that are revolutionizing so much these days, especially in the convents — the rules, I mean. When you sign yourself Bernadette, it's as though you've become my sister again, more than ever before in fact, as though I've been given back someone — or part of someone — who had been beyond my reach in a way.

Quebec City, May 2,1969

Ma chère Bernadette,

Yes, I received your sweet Easter card and your affectionate wishes, and now I also have the lovely letter you've just written me to thank you for. So I owe you a long letter in reply, which I'll try to write very soon, but do be patient a little while yet. When I came back from Florida I found a mountain of mail waiting, and all kinds of urgent little chores. Holidays always have to be paid for sooner or later. I think I'll be free before long. Another thing is that nowadays I work less quickly and it takes more effort.

Still, I must take the time to say thank you for your visits to Madame Dordu[106], and for the care you continue to give Clémence. I really want to believe that Adèle is being affectionate and attentive to her; no doubt it will be counted to her credit. I bear her no grudge, but I can't hide the fact that my heart is very heavy, for I've learned that she has made a gift of that blessed manuscript discrediting me to the archives of the Université de [. . .], where anyone can go and consult it at will. Not that she has anything very serious to reveal about me, but still, to think she'd go and personally file a kind of indictment against me in a public institution! And to think she's my godmother[107]!

Anyway, let's talk no more of it. I'm convinced that illness must be the cause of such behaviour, and I've decided I won't let myself be upset by this business any longer. Nevertheless, I learned about it from a professor at the university, who saw that blessed manuscript with his own eyes.

Dear sister, your last letter was so brimming with affection! Perhaps I should never have told you about this whole business, but I thought that Marcel, who was as shocked as could be by it all, might have mentioned it when you saw each other at the hospital last month.

But let's not make too much of it. Even this last thing can't really do me that much harm, and now we're going to put it aside for good.

Next time I hope I'll only have pleasant news for you. The summer is beginning to look very busy, however, and for the moment I don't see a chance of bringing you here. Keep praying for light at the end of the tunnel.

Much love,

Gabrielle

I enjoyed hearing that you liked Madame K.'s television lectures so much. Certainly, as you say, she's left no stone unturned to make sure my books are appreciated.

Quebec City, May 7, 1969

Ma chère Bernadette,
I said I'd never write you again about Adèle's book on me, but I have to do so once more so that you'll know all there is to know (about this business). I promise you I'll never bring it up again afterwards. It's just too awful.

The professor in question, who is writing a thesis on the Canadian novel, telephoned today to ask for an interview. He had a copy of Adèle's manuscript in front of him, the one given, as I told you, to the Université de [. . .], so that it's accessible to anyone and everyone. Having offered it to a great many publishers who didn't want it, she dreamed up this plan of placing it where it could be easily consulted. It's the culmination of a long-planned vengeance, which doesn't even benefit her materially. This professor [. . .] tells me it's a very ugly, hateful attack on me. He's offering to show it to me — though I wouldn't want to see it for anything in the world — and to write an article refuting it. I suggested that this would lend importance to Adèle's manuscript and perhaps draw more attention to it, and I didn't want that either.

There's really nothing to be done about it, I think, unless she can be persuaded to withdraw the manuscript herself, which I'm afraid she'll never do.

Dear little sister, it pains me to have to tell you such a distressing thing, but all the same, I thought you'd rather know everything involved.

I'll surely recover a certain peace of mind, but for the moment I'm dreadfully shaken.

Much love,

Gabrielle

Dear you, I'd just sealed my letter when yours arrived. I reopened mine to tell you I really don't know what to advise you, except to do as your heart tells you. I confess I'm afraid of Adèle, afraid of such a long-nurtured malice towards me.

Do as your heart tells you, and perhaps as God directs. And most of all don't be too distressed.

Fondly,

Gabrielle

Speaking to her personally might be best, if you can face it. But that's not sure to work either. I don't know what to think.

Quebec City, May 17, 1969

Ma chère Bernadette,

Yes, I think the letter you've written to Adèle takes just the right approach. You've said exactly what needs to be said. However, I fear a reaction from her that's quite the opposite of what we're hoping for[108]. I have the feeling now that she's a very sick person driven by an unrelenting urge for vengeance. Thank you anyway for all you're doing to bring her to a modicum of sense.

The professor in question [. . .] will be writing you shortly to ask you for a copy of the complete text of "Le Thème raconté"[109], which he needs for a thesis he's writing. Send him one for me, and I'd be glad if you could let me have one too.

In case you really want to form your own opinion of Adèle's manuscript, you could ask the professor for a copy, since he suggested he send me one, having the manuscript in his possession, though I didn't want to see it. It might be a good thing for you to see it yourself, though, so you'll be able to confront Adèle. According to what he tells me, it breathes hatred from beginning to end. Unfortunately I didn't think to ask the professor for his address when he came to see me yesterday, but, as I've said, he's supposed to write you about my text for Expo 67. I hope he won't take too long.

You poor dear child, how painful this tussle must be for you! As for me, it hurts so much it makes me feel nauseated. It's probably from discovering that Adèle has been preparing this attack on me for years, for there's no use trying to hide it, we have proof that it dates from long ago and hasn't lost its venom.

God help us. Do you have one of your sisters there in whom you could confide these things, and from whom you could expect good advice?

Marcel too is crushed by this whole business.

I'm praying with you, and thank you, and send you my very fondest love,

Gabrielle

Other details: the manuscript, with a letter from Adèle or delivered in person, I don't really know which, is [at the Université de X]. In the opinion of friends, [the principal] should never have accepted it in the first place. It's written under a pseudonym, Irma Deloy or Deroy.

Quebec City, May 24, 1969

Ma chère Bernadette,

Don't be too distraught over this miserable business with Adèle. There's no need to take her attacks seriously — she's a mentally unstable woman. It's a good thing if she's leaving you alone at last. If she apologizes, makes the first move towards you, I know you won't rebuff her, and that's as it should be. But don't you make the first move towards her, and whatever happens don't ever mention the name of the professor in question [. . .], even if he writes to you. She may be plaguing you now to find out details to feed her rage against this man, who has merely consulted a library document. In any case, her story that the manuscript was intended for researchers of the future doesn't stand up, because I have it from a reliable source that she offered the book to several publishers. She seems so truly sick to me that I wonder if she even remembers what she says and does from one year to the next, or from one month to the next. Anyway, it will be better for you — and even for her — if your relationship with her is a bit distant, even cut off altogether. Above all, don't take the nasty things she's been saying to you to heart, because they're just plain stupid.

Also, in case she becomes even more dangerous, keep the letter she wrote you. She was certainly unkind enough to put a private letter from me in her blessed manuscript — the only one in which I opened my heart to her a little.

Put the matter as far out of your mind as you can. Be brave, and keep on praying for all of us and looking after Clémence. Whatever Adèle says, poor child, you don't by any means live in a nice comfortable hothouse — you're so extra-sensitive you feel whatever pain the rest of us feel. You just don't make the worst of everything as she does. You keep your troubles to yourself. My fondest love to you, and I'll try to find the time to write again very soon. Thank our good friend Sister Malvina for me.

Affectionately,

Gabrielle

I gave Marcel the news about his mother's health and he thanks you. Don't say a word about any of this to Adèle, even if she comes snooping and tries to get round you, as I think she's inclined to do. Don't explain anything.

Petite-Rivière-Saint-François, June 16 [1969]

Ma chère Bernadette,
I've been dying to write you since arriving at Petite-Rivière, where the weather was magnificent for two days, even very warm for the season.

However, since yesterday it's been raining, which is very good for Marcel's little garden. Now I want to give you the latest and — I hope — final word on the case of Adèle and me — after which the matter will be closed, at least insofar as we can deal with it at the moment. A very reliable friend in Montreal [. . .], on the request of a friend of mine in Quebec City, Adrienne Choquette, herself a writer, went in person to consult "the manuscript", which oozes petty jealousy, he reports, and he persuaded the university to put it under lock and key from that day on. Unfortunately two photocopies had already been made and are in circulation [. . .]. Still, we shouldn't give too much importance to this document and the harm it could do me. Anyway, I'm promised that it will no longer be accessible to anyone (and perhaps it will be sent back to its author). I doubt that they'll go through with this last part, however. There are sensation-mongers among the faculty who may want to keep papers of that nature within reach. All the same, we have gained a lot and now I want you to stop worrying over this business; it's already caused you too much anguish. Poor dear little sister, I can see that you've taken it all terribly to heart, that you've been as badly upset by it as I was when I learned of this document's existence. It could be, as Adèle insists, that she deposited these papers for researchers later, but the intention is still the same, perhaps even worse, because it suggests she was trying to get at me from beyond the grave. Poor soul! She must really be ill to have come to such a pass, and before this to have twisted everything I've ever said or done about her, though I never had any thought of harming her as she believes I had. Now let's be done with this business. Besides, I have a cramp in my right hand — which happens often — and I can't continue. I also have pain in one foot, nothing serious, but it prevents me from walking as I like to, and since that's my principal recreation here, I'm feeling pretty frustrated. I'll try to write to Clémence very soon. In the meantime give her a hug for me if you get a chance to go and see her.

All my love,

Gabrielle

Marcel thanks you for your visits to his mother, who seems to be fairly well now.

Petite-Rivière-Saint-François, June 30, 1969

Ma chère Bernadette,
I received your sweet letter, then received one from Clémence, which was also good-natured and charming. You've both given me a great deal of pleasure, and heartache too, because I can see how much your hopes were raised, encouraged by me, about coming here this summer. Alas, as it turns out, it won't be possible. There are too many obstacles in the way. I'm not sure I can stay very long at Petite-Rivière. This business of my foot — it isn't serious, but I'll have to wear an orthopedic shoe for a while and I can't have that attended to here. I may have to go back to the city earlier than I thought. There are also all kinds of things outside my control that keep me from feeling free and available through the summer. I'm desperately sorry, and keep telling myself I'll never again go raising hopes before being almost certain of being able to realize them. To make up, do you think you could go and spend a few days somewhere with Clémence? How this pains me! But really, I just have to put off our meeting, much as we want it. You mustn't be discouraged. Either I can go and see you or you'll come here for certain next summer. Do you have a convent at Saint-Pierre, near Otterburne? When you go to see Clémence how do you get there, by bus? Or do you go by car?

I hope you won't be too bitterly disappointed by this letter. After all, next year it may still be possible and easier for us to get together. As you say, let's trust in God.

Marcel thanks you for sending news of his mother. However, now that she's better and is writing him herself, there's really no reason for you to be doing it. I know he should write more often to his relatives, and I've told him over and over, but what can I say, he's always going to resist putting pen to paper and there's nothing I can do about it. His health is perhaps a little better at the moment, but I'm afraid he'll be subject to periodic bouts of depression all his life, and not much can be done to prevent it.

I'll write soon to Clémence, but it won't be the kind of letter she's expecting, that she'd like to get and I'd so much like to have written. Goodness, how sorry I am to disappoint you both this way!

For your trips to Otterburne, for Clémence, for your own pocket money, tell me if you need anything and how much you need. There's no longer any question of my giving a cent to Adèle. She seems to get along very well without it, after all, and even finds the money to go travelling. Besides, I've come to the end of my patience with her and I'd rather hear no more of her, unless she withdraws and destroys that blasted manuscript.

Don't worry about my health. I have some little annoyances that are more hateful than serious. Keep praying the Lord to give us light, as you say, and show us the best road.

Much love,

Gabrielle

Jori sends you her kind regards. She has rented her house for the month of August, since she's leaving then for a long stay in Europe. Berthe sends her best too. Poor dear, she's exhausted from having her house full of visitors all the time. Her brother, Curé Victor, is quite ill and for the moment is staying at his little cabin.

Will you teach a few hours a day next year, or will your time be completely free?

Petite-Rivière-Saint-François, July 24, 1969

Ma chère Bernadette,

I'm so pleased with the news you gave me by phone the other day. I think the three of you are going to be totally happy at Victoria Beach[110], by that great lake. Save a place in your thoughts for me in your happiest moments.

In the midst of all your pleasure, however, be very careful not to forget Clémence's diet, and not to tempt her by putting things on the table that could make her ill, like your Paris pâté and other indigestible foods. Seriously, you must pay *great attention*, because it would be very sad if she came home ill from her holiday. Take a supply of tranquillizers too, so she'll sleep well, because the excitement could keep her awake. Make sure she takes all her medication — and now that I've said these things, go and be as happy as larks. You certainly couldn't have a better companion than Antonia[111].

I was very touched by her invitation to stay in her apartment. I'd like you to thank her very warmly for me. For the moment, with things up in the air as they are, I still can't make any decisions. Let's wait till later. It consoles me that at least the three of you will have this lovely time together at the lake, and time to rest. That's the most important thing as far as I'm concerned.

Here is $100.00 for your expenses at the lake. If there's any left, well, keep it in case you need to spend some before the end of the year. Give me a receipt if you're allowed to.

Fondest love,

Gabrielle

Petite-Rivière-Saint-François, August 17, 1969

Chère Bernadette,

Thank you for your sweet letter, which Marcel brought on the weekend. Yes indeed, as you can see I've stayed at Petite-Rivière longer than I expected, mostly because of such an awful heatwave that people can't sleep in the city. So I stayed where it was cooler, despite my foot, which is neither better nor worse but keeps me from walking much, except about once a day to Berthe Simard's — almost my only distraction. I'm lucky to have such a good neighbour. What would become of me otherwise?

Now about the Adèle business — will we ever be finished with it? — I don't think you should destroy the copy you have without authorization [from the professor]. After all, that copy became his property; he lent it to you, and without his consent you can't dispose of it. I don't really know what to think of him now, having seen him only when he came to visit me in Quebec City for a brief interview, but I don't think he intends to make use of these papers in his thesis. Not to make a big thing of them, anyway. So don't do anything without his permission. If you think it best you could ask him to give you permission to destroy them. But there will still be a copy in circulation. And then is Adèle telling the truth when she says she has taken back the manuscript? I don't think so. Perhaps the best thing, if [the professor] agrees, would be to keep his copy or make another one, which you could confront Adèle with. But to tell the truth, I no longer know what to say about this business; it's been so revolting nothing is clear any more. Trust Antonia. Her advice is good on things like this. However, it isn't really feasible to forbid universities to accept the document — or warn them about it. Just think of the number of doors a frustrated Adèle could knock on, now even more determined to "place" her manuscript. Because, barring a miracle, if she does withdraw it from one place, it'll just be to offer it somewhere else. All in all, though, as far as I can see no one really takes this "attack" seriously. So perhaps it's best for the moment to leave things alone. Particularly since, if we took the initiative with universities, archives, or others, we might seem to regard it as more important than it is. Above all we mustn't appear to be too afraid of it.

Now let's move along to other things. I'm so happy to think that next week you'll all three be at the lake. I hope with all my heart that the weather will be kind to you — not the way it is here, where it has rained every day for the past two weeks. Don't forget my suggestions about Clémence and keep an eye on her diet. With her trip to Somerset — where she'll certainly have eaten things she shouldn't have — and the excitement and everything, you'll have to watch her closely to be sure she doesn't get indigestion. Antonia should pay attention too.

You're both very lucky to have Antonia, who is so very fond of you. Give her a big hug for me, and Clémence too.

Try and be happy for all of us during the lovely week you're going to have, and offer your joy to Our Lord. We offer him our sorrows often enough. He must be pleased once in a while to receive the gift of our joy.

Affectionately,

Gabrielle

Quebec City, September 3, 1969

Ma chère Bernadette,
I read your diary-letter with the greatest pleasure. Far from boring me, so many exact details allowed me to follow you minute by minute through the beautiful true story of your holiday at Victoria Beach, first four then three of you. I'm glad for you all, but most perhaps for you and Clémence, because you've been so disappointed in your hopes for a trip and a stay in the country. You must have stored up enough good feelings to keep your souls nourished for a while. I'm so pleased you've had this week of moral and physical renewal. Money of mine was never better spent. What a pity Clémence had that cold. She's so frail, we have to be very careful she doesn't get chilled. Anyway, it's over so there's no use crying over spilt milk. Only in future, if you ever take her on a trip again, do be doubly careful she doesn't get chilled. She isn't toughened up the way you are.

I've come to town to settle a lot of small matters, also to see the doctor who's treating my foot. Whether he'll decide to operate or will want me to wear an orthopedic shoe for a few months more, I don't know for the moment. It isn't that it bothers me terribly (my foot) as long as I don't walk much. Since I really love walking, though, and it's become just about my only open-air exercise, and does me good in every way, this state of affairs is worse for me than it would be for others. Once I've finished with business matters, since the weather continues to be lovely, I'll perhaps go back to Petite-Rivière for a week if I can. We love that little place so very much, but gradually the cruel thought is gaining on us that someday we'll have to part with it, because it's too far; the trip back and forth on weekends is tiring for Marcel, and tiring for me too. Harsh reason is gradually gaining on us, flying in the face of our love for the property. Marcel is a little better, but the state of his nerves is still unstable. I confess that at times I'm worried about him and deeply discouraged, because it's his very nature that's at the root of his troubles and he doesn't seem able to change the way he lives. You've no idea what a complex person he is. Pray for him; I'm trying to help him as best I can. With people who have nervous illnesses like Marcel's, the trouble is that while they can't cure themselves they won't accept advice from people close to them. I'm counting on your kind prayers. This is all we can do for the moment.

Thank you again for such a lovely, charming letter. Take good care of yourself, and Clémence.

Much love,

Gabrielle

Quebec City, October 30, 1969

Ma chère Bernadette,
Thank you for your sweet letter. I was perhaps the first to hear the sad news of Julia's[112] death, from her granddaughter Aline, who sent me a telegram immediately. It grieved me deeply. When I stayed with her and Jos, shortly before Jos died, I came to know her well, to appreciate her and find a great deal of generosity, kindness, and love in her. Though she was perhaps a bit quick-tempered, she was extraordinarily devoted to poor Jos, who wasn't easy to live with, I'm afraid. Dear Julia, how many sleepless nights she spent beside him when he was so ill and restless, always on the verge of an asthma attack and always so apprehensive! It was no help for a heart already weakened. The little Saskatchewan village where I went to stay with Jos and Julia for a few weeks was beautiful — beautiful to me because I adored the line of hills on the horizon, the Cypress Hills, such an unexpected feature in this flat countryside. Every evening, when things weren't going too badly, Jos would sit on his little porch beside a small tree and for hours on end gaze straight ahead of him towards the mysterious folds of those hills, and then I think he was happy. It was perhaps this memory — together with many others — and the curious way in which our souls are attracted by hills, that guided me when I was writing "The Road Past Altamont"[113]. I don't know whether you've ever been in Saskatchewan — maybe not. You would have liked Dollard[114], where Papa left a piece of his heart, and which he spoke of so often. Because of Julia and the way she made me feel at home, I too have known it well. Peace to her soul. Peace to us all. In Quebec these days we are awash in the most disquieting

atmosphere of revolution and racism over the proposed language law[115]. The climate in Quebec is becoming dangerous. It's enough to make you wonder if we'll be able to live here in freedom much longer. There's a fanatic and racist demon slumbering in all peoples, and once it's unleashed it's almost impossible to catch before it's brought violence, horror, and mortal fear.

I don't want to worry you too much. The current may still be reversed, but for this we would need a dynamic leader, and we haven't got one for the time being. Dear Lord, let one appear.

I'm very pleased to hear your good news of Clémence. I'll write her soon. Take good care of her and of yourself, and as always, keep my name and Marcel's in your thoughts and your prayers. Marcel sends you his best regards.

Affectionately,

Gabrielle

Quebec City, November 24, 1969

Chère Bernadette,

I'm getting an early start on my Christmas letters, because otherwise I'll never finish. Since you're one of the first on my list, your turn has come. I wrote Clémence's letter yesterday; I hadn't written her for a good long time, I confess; today it's yours. Stirring up memories of our life as a family this way, I feel their warmth and sadness all around me. Despite the privations of our youth, yours perhaps even more than mine, it was still happier, I think, than for the young today, with all the pernicious influences and too rapid changes they're subjected to. It's never easy to grow old, I suppose, but I think it's far more difficult than ever in our own troubled times. . . . Although much good is emerging from all this commotion. . . . Here in Quebec the atmosphere is pretty stormy and sometimes I'm afraid there will be irreparable outbreaks and excesses. Unless everything is taken firmly in hand soon, I wonder if this province isn't headed for a disaster. There are times when I almost wish I were back in Manitoba.

Do tell me how you are. You never talk about that, as though you didn't want to bother others by talking about your health. Yet it's a perfectly natural subject between ourselves. What are you busy with these days? Are you completely retired? You're always so much on the go, so lively, that I can't imagine you staying idle. I suppose it's more difficult for you to visit Clémence in winter than in summer. Speaking of which, do you still have enough money for her and for yourself, which is to say, for your trips to Otterburne? Tell me frankly and I'll see what I can do. It would be better to leave it until 1970 unless you need money urgently.

Have you heard from Adèle since her last fit of temper? Poor thing, if we could only cure her of her persecution complex! Eliane[116], who was in Quebec City staying with her daughter Céline, who's married to Michel de Repentigny, gave me some news of her . . . which wasn't too bad, really. But it's true that Eliane, who's so tactful and kind, skips cleverly over anything unpleasant and tries to patch things up in her good-natured way. She came in September. I don't remember if I've told you since then about her visit, which I really enjoyed because her daughter Céline, who's very nice, took all of us, me, her mother, and the children, by car to Les Ecureuils, a pretty village on the river, where the ancestral home of the Toupins of Saint-Boniface is located. Eliane's interest in the house, which is nearly three hundred years old and magnificent, is due to the fact that one of her sons, Rhéal, I think, married a Toupin descended from the family that lived in this very house. Anyhow, we had a delightful drive on an autumn day of spectacular colours, and it was a joy to listen to Eliane, inspired by the occasion, telling us all kinds of things about the history, family life, and past of our people. But she must have told you all about this drive when she returned, at least I hope she did, because I know how you love to get news fresh from the oven, so to speak.

In any event, you'll probably have the joy of seeing Jean, Yolande, and the children soon, because it seems that when they come back to Canada they will go straight to Manitoba to spend Christmas and New Year's. So you'll likely get to give them a hug before I do. I can't wait to see the children in particular. After Julia died, I received very lovely letters — as I think I already wrote you — from Blanche and her daughter Aline[117]. These letters show an extreme and delicate sensitivity, the Roy sensitivity, I'd call it, a quality that's a characteristic of our family, and which I recognize by its tenderness, vibrancy, and anguish. Our father had it, and it remains alive in many of his children. How marvellous it is to find it still in young Aline!

My dear Dédette, as Christmas approaches, since I probably won't have time to write you again before, I'm sending you a great big hug and wishing you peace of mind — of which you have more already than most people, but it's something we can all use more of, isn't it? Wishing you good health as well, and some good times with Clémence. I shall be with you both fondly in my thoughts.

All my love,

Gabrielle

P.S. Dear little sister. My letter was ready to go when yours arrived. I think Clémence is right, really — sad though it may be — not to want to get too close again to Adèle, who is too disruptive and upsetting for her, which does no one any good. So invite her to the convent if it's possible; with you she'll spend a nice, quiet, happy Christmas. I'll write to Rodolphe[118] one of these days, forcing myself to the extreme. Not that I haven't forgiven him; I've done so wholeheartedly. But the letters I've had from him, and news I've had of him, have disturbed me so profoundly that each time I've had the greatest difficulty regaining my composure — which really is very fragile. But I'll try. . . . I must confess to you that a few years ago Rodolphe was doing the rounds of my friends and acquaintances — including Marcel and his sister Léona, without my knowledge, asking for money. But for me these are such painful memories, let's try to forget them. My foot, unfortunately, isn't better at all. Quite the contrary. I can only just manage to do my little bit of shopping in the nearest stores. What's more, the orthopedic shoes don't help in the least. The doctor who is treating me seems reluctant to operate, perhaps fearing that the operation won't bring any improvement. Sometimes I'm [really alarmed][119], the thought crossing my mind that perhaps I'm becoming a cripple. Not being able to walk as much as I like seems almost as cruel as going deaf or blind. Moreover, I have the impression that I'm not getting the care I should. That's the way it always is with doctors' wives; they have to see their husbands' colleagues, who, for fear of being caught making a wrong diagnosis, are too timid to try anything at all . . . so the shilly-shallying goes on for ever. Say a prayer for me. I think it will be paradise if I can just have the joy of walking freely in the country again.

Much love once again,

Gabrielle

I'd like to go to Arizona if I can. Because of this foot, I simply don't know for the moment. As for Marcel, there's no point at all trying to persuade him to come too. If he has free time in winter he always goes to visit his mother. And then he's not keen on spending any time in the United States. How sweet of you to give a birthday party for Clémence! Thank you.

Quebec City, December 4, 1969

Chère Bernadette,
I'm replying immediately as you asked me to. Of course you may take some of the money at your disposal for pocket money on the trip if you decide to go to Vancouver. As for the trip, I don't know what to advise you. Clémence is quite right not to want to go. At her age, frail as she is, it would be asking for trouble. I don't want to worry you unduly, but if you left on such a long trip with Clémence you'd risk having to cope if she fell ill on the way. For yourself it's different, and I imagine whatever you decide will be right. However, don't forget that Rodolphe[120] had you and Anna come to him before, saying he was at death's door, and it was far from being the case. Perhaps he really is much worse this time. It's possible. But he has so often cried wolf that people aren't inclined to take his distress signals seriously any more. Besides, if he were as ill as he says, would he be in any condition to set himself up as he has? It all seems a bit odd to me. However, if your heart tells you to go and your community will pay for your ticket, why not go, after all? Our cousin

Eva[121] is there — I don't know whether you have her address; she could probably find a convent where you could stay,because you'd need to arrange that before leaving, and if possible it shouldn't be too far from where Rodolphe lives. Dear child, you're just like the rest of us, drawn by the idea of going somewhere, of travelling, of far horizons, as well as by the ties of blood. So don't fret over it any longer, go where you think you'll be the most help. And when you do you'll see those high Rocky Mountains of yours again, which so deeply moved you when you first saw them. Don't worry too much about my foot. In the end I'll probably find a doctor who'll be able to clear up this nuisance for me. That's what really prevented me from being able to have you and Clémence last summer, that and in a way lack of space as well.

As far as Adèle is concerned, you're probably right to make the first move towards her, although she's the one who offended you so it's really up to her to do it, but no matter, it's never dumb to be the first to forgive. Only do promise me you'll be on your guard with her, because I truly believe her to be incurably ill with envy and it's an illness that can drive her to acts of pure spite, as we've seen. So for the love of heaven, keep your wits about you. And don't get Clémence going to Adèle's again. It always turns out badly when she takes to seeing Adèle too often. Adèle gets her all churned up with her endless arguments. You're impulsive and it's part of your charm, but when you've learned a lesson once, do try to remember it. It's one thing to forgive but quite another to put our trust in someone whom experience has taught us not to trust. So be cautious with Adèle. Something tells me we haven't seen the last of her evil plans, and she surely hasn't given up as a result of your prayers, quite the contrary. Don't go and mistake the wishes of your generous heart for reality.

Well now, if you do decide to go to Vancouver, let me know. And go with joy and without a worry, if this is what your heart tells you.

Affectionately,

Gabrielle

March — April 1970

Quebec City, March 6, 1970

Chère Bernadette,

Could you follow up on what the writer of the enclosed letter wants? By giving it to Adèle? Replying yourself? I'd be grateful. I had an operation on my foot seven weeks ago and have begun to walk outside a little each day. I'm not sure my right foot, the other one, isn't threatening to go the way of the left. Let's hope it's something else, but there are some aggravating little symptoms. I'm still waiting for more complete news of your trip to Vancouver. My poor little sister, I'm afraid things there weren't very pleasant for you, but you were right all the same to follow the bidding of your kind heart and your urge to travel. I'll write you at more length later because for the moment — is it the sedatives I've taken? — my mind seems to be horribly empty. Would you give me Antonia's telephone number? I seem to have lost it.

Much love,

Gabrielle

How is our Clémence?

Quebec City, March 9, 1970

Ma chère Bernadette,
I hope this letter reaches you. I'm not sure it will because, with this postal strike in Montreal, mountains of mail accumulate and stay there in heaps indefinitely. But with luck this letter may slip through. I so wish I could be by your side when you're suffering so — I really sensed it last night in your poor little voice. I'm praying with all my heart that they'll find the cause of your pain right away and be able to remedy it without delay[122]. I'm so glad Antonia[123] is there; she has promised to keep me informed. What would we do without her? So kind, so generous, a real sister to us. A few days ago I wrote you an unimportant few lines about a request concerning Adèle, whose address I don't have. It was just before I learned you were ill. Don't bother yourself about it. Perhaps Antonia could write a brief reply about Adèle to that letter from Edmonton.

I'm praying for your pain to be relieved quickly. Poor dear child, to me your voice has always been so vibrant, as if charged with electrical waves, and yesterday I couldn't get over hearing it so faint and far away. Still, I was relieved to be able to exchange a few words with you. This is just a quick line dashed off and sent hastily in hope it will arrive quickly, bringing you all our love, mine and Marcel's. If there's anything you need, let us know through Antonia.

A great big loving hug and kiss to you,

Gabrielle

Quebec City, March 10, 1970

Ma chère Bernadette,
You're in pain and I can't relieve your suffering — how this hurts me! But at last I've received your lovely, brave letter written from your hospital bed. Dear sister, I admire you for finding the strength to write

me when you're in such pain, and even to think of reassuring me. We're surrounded by suffering, but also by beauty and kindness. How strange it all is indeed! Pain is never far away, it's true, and remains our perpetual enemy. Yet there are those who would take on themselves the pain suffered by others if they could. I'm praying with all my heart that yours will leave you at last. I'm hoping you'll soon be cured, soon be able to write me one of your lovely letters as only you can write them, so vibrant, so lyrical. Dear heart, I would give a great deal to be beside you and holding your hand, at least. Our little mother must be watching over you now with special tenderness from up there in the sky. She loved you so much, was so proud of her "beautiful Dédette". Incidentally, I did receive that photograph of you that I've always loved, the one where you look so proud. Do you know what gives you that look of pride? Well, I think it has something to do with your nostrils — they almost seem to quiver.

With much love,

Gabrielle

Quebec City, March 12, 1970

Ma chère Bernadette,

I hope my poor letters are being some help to you at least. I can do so little for you at the moment and this distresses me. Since Antonia hasn't telephoned again I'm concluding that your trouble isn't worse and that things may even have improved. Late yesterday afternoon I went into the church, the one next door to our apartment house. I stayed for the five o'clock mass and prayed fervently to our Creator — Maman as well — to help you. I often ask Maman for help this way; she did so much for us on earth, dear soul, and I think she can still do something for us.

As for me, I gain some ground each day. I now have real hope that I'll walk again as I used to. I still have some sharp pains at night, but it's nothing compared to what I endured before. The postal strike has begun again intermittently in Montreal and my letters to you, which I'm sending often these days — this is the third this week — are perhaps being delayed, which cuts me to the heart. It's a sad time when harsher and harsher tensions affect people to the point where they come to the end of their tether.

If your pain leaves you any respite — and how I hope it does! —your thoughts must roam far and wide, coming and going from one horizon to another, making discoveries, for when we are ill we are led to explore every side of the mystery in which we live, don't you find? I'm so impatient to hear that you've taken a turn for the better. Yesterday I received a lovely letter from Clémence, who had learned by telephone from Adèle that you were ill and was hastening to tell me, not realizing that I knew already. I dropped her a line as soon as I received her letter, hoping to keep her from feeling too lonesome. Poor little soul, she seems to be resigning herself to her lot and is beginning to like the home at Otterburne. It's thanks to you that she's there and in good hands, and we can never thank you enough for this.

I'll write again soon, dear little sister. Marcel sends you his affectionate regards.

A big hug from us both,

Gabrielle

Quebec City, March 14, 1970

Ma chère Bernadette,

I telephoned Antonia yesterday and she told me how you were doing. I was so pleased when she told me your morale was better. When you've got through a few more difficult days, you should start recovering quite quickly. This is what I've been asking most urgently of the Creator. I took communion for you and spoke to Maman's soul, beseeching her to stay close to you and help you endure the trial you're going through. I'd fly to your side if I thought my presence would be useful, but let's wait a little if you think, as I do, that we'd take more pleasure in being together once you've begun to return to health. In any event, Antonia and your kind Sister Superior, with whom I had a long talk about you on the telephone, have both promised to keep in close touch with me. So don't be too worried. There are plenty of us to keep an eye on you, to care for you constantly. I found Sister Valcourt[124] — is this the way to spell her name? — wonderfully understanding and extremely fond of you. It did me a lot of good to open my heart to her. I feel I've known her for ever. It must be a great joy for you to owe obedience to such a benevolent authority, who applies the authority she has with such a gentle hand. When we see such things we have to admit that the Church's reforms are a great improvement, in spite of some excesses and some real folly, but at least it's not as bad as the rigidity there was before. Surely it's better to have some acknowledged weaknesses than a façade that has lost all warmth and life.

My dear, dear Bernadette, as I wrote in an earlier letter, the most inescapable pain in life is perhaps in not being able to relieve others of pain, not being able to take it on oneself for a time at least to allow some rest to those who suffer. But who knows, perhaps this miracle can happen without our noticing. So I'm going to pray and have prayers said for your pain to cease, and for you to know the sweet feeling of well-being that comes when pain subsides. Marcel sends you his most affectionate regards. Both of us, in fact, are staying close beside you in our thoughts.

My fondest love,

Gabrielle

[March 22 or 23, 1970][125]

A ma chère Dédette,
A carnation from my birthday bouquet, with my warmest thanks for the beautiful birthday celebration you directed from your hospital bed, the way Napoleon directed his great battles from his bivouac.

Tenderly, sleep well tonight.

Gabrielle

Quebec City, April 8, 1970

Ma chère Bernadette,
I had as good a return trip as was possible in the circumstances. My thoughts never left you. A picture of you travelled with me in my mind. I saw you most of all on Easter Sunday, sitting in your easy chair, looking majestic in your new-style veil that's so becoming, and with your mantle or rather shawl around your shoulders, receiving visitors with that manner you have of giving of yourself, your whole self, with all the verve you've accustomed us to. Thank you for that lovely Easter party, which went off as smoothly as could be, thanks to you. I also saw you walking on my arm along the main hallway of the convent, sometimes lifting your feet high as in a ceremonial goosestep, you dear little soldier of love and brotherhood. And I never stop seeing your beautiful eyes, grey like the clouds today. Although I saw you suffering — so valiantly — I've told you that already and I'm telling you again because nothing is more true — my visits to the hospital and then to the convent, in fact all the hours I spent with you over those three weeks, are now for me like a huge book filled with lessons and rich memories, or, if you like, an audio tape where everything we talked about is recorded, and all the confidences we exchanged.

Today I'm starting on the covenant of prayer we made, and I shall ask for your well-being — as you will ask for mine, I hope — with all my love and also with all the confidence in God that you have helped me acquire. I shall ask him most especially to grant you sweet, sound sleep. Perhaps you would like me to recall once more the opening lines of Baudelaire's "Invitation to Travel", which you seemed to like so much when I recited them for you.

> My child, my sister,
> If only we two
> Could live in that land afar
> With time to love
> To love and die
> Where all is the way you are.[126]

For our very dear Sister Valcourt, for Sister Rose, for Sister Monique, those unforgettable, sweet, loving faces all around you, I feel my heart overflow with gratitude. For their tenderness towards you, for their extraordinary kindness towards me. I shall write to each of them when I've cleared away some of the mountain of mail I found awaiting me.

Marcel is well and sends you a hug in his great strong arms and a big kiss on each cheek.

A hug and kiss from me as well with all my love. I shall be at mass for you at Saint Dominique Church at a quarter past five this afternoon.

> Good night sweet Prince
> May flight[s] of angels sing thee to thy rest.

It was really more like spring in Manitoba than it is here, where there's still a nip in the air. So, along with my picture of you, a breath of spring is my parting memory of my visit to Manitoba.

Au revoir, my Dédette.

Gabrielle

Quebec City, April 9, 1970

Ma chère Bernadette,
I'm going to try to write you every day, hoping my letters will reach you without delay in spite of the persisting postal slowdown. I'd like them to fly straight to you like the birds of spring, bearers of my love for you, the tenderness I feel for you, which kept growing in the three weeks I spent with you as I came to know you better. It's still cold here. Yesterday evening there was even a tentative little snowstorm, which came to nothing fortunately.

And I still haven't heard the crows, a sure sign for me that summer is coming. When I so love to hear them in April, to think that I get so I could shoot them at Petite-Rivière when they come and sit in the birch trees and wake me at four in the morning!

Yesterday evening I began attending mass for you in Saint Dominique Church, just a step away from here. There are never many people at this mass at the end of the day. There were perhaps forty of us, scattered here and there like shadows in that huge nave, yet I felt a profound faith uniting these souls who knew nothing of each other. I don't know if I really prayed, but I sat with the others and let my thoughts flow like water towards our Supreme Friend, and I felt a kind of peacefulness come over me. Perhaps you were responsible for this through your prayers.

I never stop thinking of those lovely conversations we had on all kinds of subjects, of your dear sisters at the convent, how they enveloped me with their caring, and how different they really are from what we in the world imagine — how full their lives are, and how rich, generous, and giving, in contrast to what is sometimes said of them. In any event, I don't think I've met many people as unfailingly kind as Sister Berthe Valcourt, or many women on whom you can rely in all confidence as you can on Sister Rose Desrochers. If I hadn't seen you cared for and loved by these women before coming away, I really would have been too distressed to leave you there. Now I know that you'll be given every care, and this at least soothes my worries.

Marcel is delighted to know that you're pleased with the little gilded icon. Although he bought it in Greece, in Athens, he thinks it's of Russian origin and must depict the Virgin of Wisdom, or something like that. Anyway he's sure this Mary is not a young woman, and though not really old is steeped in a profound wisdom of the world, has lived long and knows much about the suffering of souls, yet is more certain than ever that happiness awaits us in the end. May she watch over you, protect you, and tonight and in nights to come bring you sound, peaceful sleep. Do trust in our natural mother too. I sometimes think that even though she's at peace, if there's still a mite of anxiety in her heart it's for us, her children, and she still watches over us with the same tenacity she put into protecting us on earth. This evening I shall be joining you at the same time as yesterday, at Saint Dominique Church.

Meanwhile, a big hug and my fondest love to you,

Gabrielle

Have the angel musicians been back to play chamber music in your chamber?

Quebec City, April 10, 1970

Mon enfant, ma soeur,

Yesterday, hunting in my messy old papers and the notebooks in which I've been keeping choice thoughts for ages, I found the Hindu prayer I was trying to remember and couldn't when I was with you. Here it is:

> Lead me from the unreal to the real,
> from the dark into the light,
> from death to immortality.

As for that other thought, from the Bhagavad-Gita, I didn't recite it quite right. Here is the way it goes:

> And all creatures
> are in me as in
> a great ceaseless wind
> moving in space.

Then there's this marvellous Chinese proverb:

> A great tree attracts much wind.

And this Sanskrit proverb:

> The tree casts its shade upon all,
> even upon the woodcutter.

And then, by Bernanos, this lovely definition of art:

> It cannot be denied: art has an end other than itself. Its perpetual search for expression is only a pale image, something like the symbol, of its perpetual search for Life.

So there's my little harvest of thoughts gleaned just for you. As you can see, creative artist or nun in a convent, it's really the same thing we keep searching for, the same goal that keeps us moving forward.

I've just written to Clémence and then to Sister Berthe. At the rate of two or three letters a day — besides my ordinary correspondence —I'm gradually writing my thank-you notes expressing the gratitude I owe to your wonderful sisters at the convent, to my hostesses, Léa, Eliane, and Antonia, to all those friends and loving relatives who took such good care of me when I was in Saint-Boniface that I've brought back some unforgettable memories of them. But my most beautiful and lasting memory is of you. You already occupied a big place in my heart, though I wasn't fully or even partly aware of it. Now, all of a sudden, that place is enormous. And suddenly I've realized that I've always had, and always will have, only one real sister, one who is really close, with the same likes and dislikes, the same ideals and identical inclinations, and this sister who is so very close is you, Dédette my dear.

God bless you!

Yesterday began the second phase of the path of prayer each of us is following for the other. Would you believe it, there in the almost deserted church I suddenly felt at peace, consoled and protected in a certain mysterious way. The thought came to mind that it was you who had won me this feeling of comfort. I hope with all my heart that I can win it for you as well.

My love to you.
Also Marcel's.
Au revoir, my dear Dédette.

Gabrielle

Quebec City, April 11, 1970

Ma chère "Dédette",
Why haven't I dared call you this before? It's a name I've always loved for you. There was Sister Léon-de-la-Croix, who was certainly caring and affectionate, but to my youthful eyes a bit distant, and she kept me at a distance. Then Bernadette came back and was so much closer, as tender-hearted as Sister Léon, the same person really, but so familiar all of a sudden because of her name, my own little sister, one I could feel free to play jokes on. And now that you're ill, now that I've been able to do small, unimportant things for you, I have my Dédette back again, just the way she was when I was a child. Better than ever in fact. For my Dédette is now even gentler, even more forgiving, and her heart is now so tender I can't imagine how it could be more so.

Today I'm going to mass at a quarter to twelve for you. I like the five o'clock mass better, I find it so suffused with the peacefulness and beauty of the end of the day, but Marcel and I are going out for some fresh air and relaxation this afternoon, and in case I don't get back in time I'm playing it safe and going earlier to pray for you. For you or for me? Perhaps it comes to the same thing. One way or the other, may God grant us what he knows we need the most. You see, I'm doing as you asked me to — I'm leaving everything in his hands.

I've sent a book to each of your delightful nurses, Sister Rose and Sister Monique. I hope they'll be pleased.

The weather is still terrible here, much more like autumn than the end of winter. And I miss the great light-filled sky, the tall Manitoba sky, now that I've rediscovered its beauty. What a sky it is! Perhaps there's none clearer anywhere in the world, except Greece. If even there. When all is said and done, I'm not sure the Manitoba sky isn't the more magical of the two for me.

May the Lord God grant you a sound sleep, tonight and every night.

All my love,

Gabrielle

Quebec City, April 12, 1970

Ma chère Dédette,

Did I at least thank you properly for the lovely birthday party you organized for me, ill as you were, with such care, attention, and generosity? I think it was the loveliest birthday party of my whole life. It had everything, a cake with my name on it, a bouquet of carnations — my favourite flowers — true friends around me, and pervading all of this, the vital presence of your love bringing life to everything around, penetrating the walls of your hospital room to find and envelop me with warmth [wherever I was]. During this meal that you had asked for and planned, I confess I often had trouble swallowing because of the lump in my throat. Thank you, thank you, thank you again my dearest Dédette. You've always had, and you have more and more, a flair for creating unforgettable moments. You invariably put the mark of your personality on them, your love, the way an artist puts his mark on things. And ever after, people see in them what you have seen.

I hope you've seen the truth as well in this: that when Adèle received the money from *you*, her heart softened and her attitude improved.

As for me, I continue to keep the precious pact of love and prayer that we made; I'm in the fifth day and for me it's bringing a mysterious peacefulness, although I still worry terribly about you and grieve to have seen you in such pain. It's a peacefulness that seems to come to me from far, far away, from some immense source beyond everything we know through reason and the senses, through logic. And therein resides the only whole, total truth, towards which we have been walking all our lives, without really knowing it.

I'm writing to just about everyone to give them your news, as I imagine it's tiring for you to write to so many people. So I've written to Bob asking him to give Rodolphe the news, to Blanche Roy, to Yolande Cyr[127]. I've also given your regards to the Madeleines, who were very touched and are going to write you. I hope Antonia comes to see you often. You only need let her know when you'd like her to come, because she has told me she'll be available to you at any time. She's so fond of you. Who isn't, for that matter? Perhaps the success of a person's life is measured by the intensity of love it has inspired in others. If this is so, then yours is a total success, for with my own eyes I have seen a rare degree of love in the eyes of children, your sisters at the convent, the nephews and nieces, and everyone who knows you, and I think I know something about observation.

Sleep now if it's possible, my dear Dédette, sleep shielded from your pain, sleep in peace. I'm wishing for this so hard, it isn't possible for me not to gain it for you.

It gives me such pleasure to write you every day. It's become a pleasant routine, if I may say so, one to which I turn my first attentions of the day, my first thoughts as soon as I'm up.

Marcel sends you much love. He's not much for letter-writing, but he thinks of you often all the same, and with great affection.

I'll be writing again soon, Dédette mine.

Gabrielle

Quebec City, April 13, 1970

Ma chère Dédette,
This morning at last I heard the crows in the sky announcing spring, and it awakened the memory of water flowing, buds swelling at the ends of branches, all the revival that grips our hearts each time as if it were the first.

How happy it made me to hear your voice yesterday morning on the telephone — you've no idea! It was a wonderful present. Marcel was getting dressed in his room next to mine. Suddenly he heard me say "Dédette" and rushed in, all excited, so he could say hello to you too. There are moments like this for which we could pour blessings on the telephone, forgetting all the annoyance it can bring us at other times. Sister Rose told me you had had a fairly good night, and this was a great comfort too. We've come to the middle of our program of prayer together, and I find such tranquillity and hope through it that I'm not about to say I won't continue once we've completed it. Praying for someone else is better than praying for oneself in the first place, there's no doubt. This makes me think of something Simone Weil once said, that while there's more benefit in correcting oneself than correcting others, most people just work at correcting others.

I was so happy yesterday to talk to you on the telephone — I keep coming back to this — to talk to you and Sister Monique and Sister Rose and our irreplaceable Sister Berthe, who must have come running because they'd no sooner said, "They've gone to fetch Sister Superior" than there she was at the other end, talking to me. I really felt I was among friends, as every time I've been to visit you at the convent. All their concern for you at least softened the hurt I felt at leaving you.

This week I should be receiving a lot of letters, because last week I wrote dozens — from Wednesday on at any rate. Thank-you notes to those who put me up, or helped me in any number of ways, and to you, of course. But in your case I don't expect you to answer because I know what an effort it takes and I'd be just as pleased to know that you're getting as much rest as possible. So let me chatter away alone at my end and don't worry about replying.

It's joyously sunny today and I'm going to try to find the time to go for a short walk outside, although I have a bit of pain again in the foot that was operated on, which I don't understand at all because it was better while I was in Manitoba. Perhaps it will go when I've had some exercise, or perhaps I don't yet have the kind of shoes I should.

Did you go to the little infirmary dining room this morning? I try to imagine your comings and goings and what you're doing, so I'll feel closer to you, and I'm endlessly grateful nowadays to have had all those visits with you, because I came to know so much about your daily life that now I can follow you about in my thoughts almost all day long. So not an ounce of the love and understanding we have for others in this world is ever wasted.

Marcel sends his affectionate thoughts and I my fondest love to you.

Gabrielle

Quebec City, April 14, 1970

Ma chère Dédette,
I find it so comforting to be keeping our compact of prayer that I'm going to suggest, since this one finishes on April 16, that we begin another at once, the day after. Then there will be no interruption in this bond between us, whose power and effectiveness I can feel even at this distance, and which, I hope with all my heart, helps you as it helps me. So I'm going to mass at a quarter past five every evening. There aren't many people, but the atmosphere is none the less warm and fraternal, as well as prayerful. All kinds of things go through my mind, a great many memories of us, of our family. It's an odd way to pray, perhaps. Still, I don't see why God wouldn't be pleased to see us at rest in his church, relaxed and daydreaming.

It's a beautiful day today, a real spring day. In the country, the water in the brooks must be singing. How I'd love to be pushing you outside in your wheelchair where you could take deep breaths of the bracing air and look at the sky. You can see the sky from your room, I know, above the fields between the convent and where the skating rink was when I was young. This is one view of Saint-Boniface at least that hasn't changed, and remains faithful to our early memories. But it doesn't matter if old memories are carried off with traces of the past, as long as our hearts stay young, and our hearts are young as long as they're confident. And I marvel at yours, it's still so full of excitement and the thrill of life, like a child's, or a bird's — still a loving heart as well, which has throbbed so intensely it's a wonder it has so much intensity left.

Much love,

Gabrielle

Quebec City, April 15, 1970

Ma chère Dédette,

I'm correcting my article, "Mon héritage du Manitoba", which will appear in *Manitoba in Literature*, to be published by the University of Manitoba as a special issue of the magazine *Mosaic*[128]. Which is to say, I'm correcting the proofs they've just sent me. There will probably be some excerpts from *The Road Past Altamont* as well. They've made quite a lot of typographical errors, so I was well advised to ask for a set of proofs to correct.

I have plenty to keep me busy these days. But that doesn't stop my thoughts from turning constantly to you. It doesn't stop me from seeing your face in my mind's eye. I often see you when I was making you laugh, with your hands on your stomach and your mouth slightly open, making a little O to protect your incision from the jolting caused by laughing — I see all this and I want to laugh and cry at the same time. What a dauntless spirit a human being has! Knowing it will hurt more if we laugh, we laugh anyway because we see what is comical in everything and in spite of everything.

How I'd love to be with you still, telling you those crazy little anecdotes that made you laugh. Like Alphonse Allais[129] making a double pun with "*Mon merdecin mirlitaire*"; or saying to the station-master, "With your pretty little country station you'd be a smash hit in Paris."

It was you who inspired me to tell those stories, you know, and to find those things in the back of my memory, by listening so warmly and totally. Being listened to like that always brings out the entertainer in one. Dear Dédette, what full, rich hours I spent with you, filled with the joy of coming to know you better, and an affection which I believe was deepening from day to day. So what we had was a real coming together, and it left us with a feeling of discovery, at least it did for me. We may think we know others, but we can always learn more about them. From you, from the way you put up with your ordeal, your illness, I've learned a lesson in courage like few others in my life. My thought is that you are as dear to God's heart as any thing of beauty he has created in this world — flowers, the sunset, dawn, the song of a bird, the wind, or waving grasses. I'm in no doubt whatever that he loves and treasures you infinitely. I'm so certain of this I can see it written, graven, proclaimed in everything. It's spelled out in the tall sky of Manitoba. So take courage if your pain returns in force. It will go away again, be sure of it.

And now I must repeat something I've told you before, and that's how much I love to remember the sound of your voice on the telephone, saying that you were offering *everything* to God for me.

At mass, today again, I shall offer him *everything* for you.

My fondest love,

Gabrielle

Quebec City, April 16, 1970

Chère Dédette,

The path of prayer we have been walking together ends today, but I'm beginning again tomorrow, as I've already told you, because at this time I can't face not staying as close beside you as I possibly can, or not feeling that you're close beside me. This fraternity of our souls is too beautiful to be broken. So let's both begin again. I don't understand any better what place pain has in creation, and knowing that you're in pain still grieves me as much as before, but I think I can see how pain is the tool with which we're forged — or with which we forge ourselves —and joy as well, for that matter. Pain and joy: life is a terrible pendulum swinging between these two extremes.

I'm glad to hear that Clémence came to see you, and also our cousins Léa and Eliane[130]. It was very good of Antonia to run the errand I asked her to do for me and I'm pleased you like the flowers. I'm pleased most of all with your letter, which arrived this morning; so typical of you, you know, so grateful for the smallest thing anyone does for you, and vibrant, always, like the leaves on a poplar, like the surface of water touched by a breath of wind. Of the countless marvels of nature, not a thing is lost on you. You have sensed every one of them, carried them in your heart and cherished them, and he who created them for us must be well pleased with you. For above all he must love to see us love his universe.

I'm going to pray specially for you to have a better sleep tonight.

My fondest love to you,

Gabrielle

Jean Palmer telephoned me yesterday from her house in Les Eboulements, having heard from the Madeleines that you were ill. She asked me to remember her to you with special friendship. She hasn't in the least forgotten your liveliness, your unique personality, and still warmly recalls the calendar decorated with birchbark that you made for her, "One of the most precious gifts I've ever received," she says. I told her your remark that it was a gift that even a millionairess had been delighted with, and she laughed and laughed . . . with affection... and pleasure.

G.

Quebec City, April 17, 1970

Ma très chère Dédette,
It's really quite astonishing that you should think of my letters as a shield that protects you, because this is exactly what I hoped they would be, this is why I write them, so they'll form a kind of buffer zone around you through which nothing bad can pass. I've always felt that this must be the most important effect of the love we have for others, and perhaps it's also the secret of what we call the community of saints, a great circle of souls each striving to help the others, with the Lord in the centre.

But how I wish this could help you sleep reasonably well at night. I know so well how wretched it is to lie awake, trying to fight it but feeling utterly alone. Yet it's not our night-time thoughts that speak the truth and must be heeded, it's those that return in calm and relaxation with the dawn of day. But we do have to get through the night if we're going to recognize the dawn of day, don't we?

I've had a sweet letter from Berthe Simard asking after you with concern. Every time she writes she tells me she has the most pleasant and lasting memories of you and Clémence visiting Petite-Rivière. How indeed could anyone forget the tiny figure in nun's black and white, hurrying up hill and down dale and stopping to talk to everyone, so elated with her freedom and the joy of living that it was a mighty good lesson to us all.

I see by the weather reports that it's Manitoba's turn to suffer another attack of winter, while here it's turned mild at last.

With my inward eye I often picture your little room, your table and armchair, the rocking chair you had brought for me, the stool I moved for you a hundred times, the big window overlooking a bit of open space and the sky. And you, most of all you, with your little white cap just a bit crooked and your little hand with its gentle index finger extended, and the others curled under like the foot of a bird. I see you always busy thinking of others, writing a note, sending yet another present, having one knitted by "one of our sisters", always and endlessly giving, giving, giving. So it is that while you've never really possessed anything of your own, you've given more than anyone else. This is the magic of Dédette — having nothing of her own yet always finding something to give.

Did I tell you I telephoned Yolande to let her know what I'm up to these days? The angel for Gisèle hadn't yet arrived but Gisèle will surely be delighted and will write and thank you without fail. It's so sweet and so right for her age and tastes, a present she surely won't ever forget.

God bless you, "my child, my sister", and grant you sound sleep tonight.

Lovingly,

Gabrielle

I have a friend who is burdened these days with woes I won't name; I've told her I would put her case under your protection, in your hands. Say a prayer for her please, Dédette mine.

Quebec City, April 18, 1970

Ma chère Dédette,

Coming back to your phrase "a shield that protects you" in your beautiful, inspiring letter, it continues to amaze me. This is truly what is achieved by human love; love alone can create protection around the loved one, the one to be defended. Moreover, at the same time that you're feeling protected through my prayers, through your prayers I too feel a kind of peacefulness, for all my intense grief to know that you're so ill. I feel this particularly in church, during the mass I'm attending in your name and for you. Still, I've come to feel intensely nostalgic for that time I spent in Saint-Boniface, when I could see you so often and each time feel enriched by being near you, even though it upset me terribly to see you suffer so.

After a delightful spring day yesterday, the sky is cloudy today, but the air is still warm. I've begun to take some pleasure in walking again, though not too far all at once. So I'm getting used to taking two or three short walks a day rather than one long one in the afternoon.

It's good this way because I get different views of the day. I talk to you constantly while I walk, as indeed I do at home. As soon as I'd left Saint-Boniface I began having a kind of inner conversation with you, and it almost never stops. I tell you this and that, and you listen, always with such interest in my imagination that it stimulates me to tell you more and more. So we're always together. Not one thought crosses my mind that I don't share at once with you. It would take a great big book to hold it all, and there's so much crowding into my mind that I'd never get it all down, either. So you're involved in every moment of my life, even the most inconsequential. Yesterday, for instance, we had some excellent vegetable soup, and I enjoyed it, but I was sad as well because I couldn't have a bowl of it brought to you, though I kept thinking it would have stimulated your poor little appetite and you would have eaten it with relish. Silly thoughts, perhaps, yet they're important in their way, and I'd have given a lot to have had you taste my soup. Many is the time I also think of our dearest Sister Valcourt, whose kindness, thoughtfulness, and generosity towards us both I shall never forget. What a wealth there is in her!

My Dédette, my dearest wish for you, today as every day, is for you to have a good night's sleep, a sweet, restful sleep.

All my love to you,

Gabrielle

Quebec City, April 19, 1970

Ma chère, chère Dédette,

What a delight to have talked to you on the telephone this morning! Your dear voice coming from so far away touched my heart deeply. You're right, we'll never be apart. People who really love each other can't be. I have another compact to suggest, and it's this: whichever one of us reaches heaven first will forevermore take care of the one still on earth. The Lord will grant her this easily, because it must be what he most wishes for in his creatures — the kind of love between them that nothing can destroy or diminish. That beautiful, prophetic photograph of the two of us showed long ago that we were close and always would be close[131]. I know you'll never fail me and you can be sure I won't ever fail you.

Meanwhile, I'm continuing my second novena of prayer for you, my Dédette. I'm going to take communion for you at the five o'clock mass today.

Marcel has promised to come to this mass and pray for you too. We'll all three be together, as you have so dearly wished.

"My child, my sister, if only we two could live in that land afar...."

All my love,

Gabrielle

Quebec City, April 20, 1970

Ma très chère Dédette,

All day yesterday, after talking to you on the telephone, I kept hearing the sound of your voice in me, and this morning as I sit here writing you I hear it again, as though it will always be with me. And what I hear you say most often is, "We'll never be apart. We'll always be together as we are in the photograph." Dear heart, as always you've found the right words to comfort and encourage me. I look at this dear little picture, the only one that's gone with me everywhere for years, and realize I'm just beginning now to understand the indescribable, mysterious attraction it has for me. There's a reason why I've loved it since the day I found it, and why I love it more and more as the years go by. It's because it guarantees me a greater love and protection than I've ever had before, one that couldn't ever fail me. In your arms I look like a frail little bird that you want to protect from adversity. Now you're the one who is the battered bird, the prey of illness, and I'm the one trying to protect you with my prayers and all the yearning of my soul. But the roles will be reversed the moment your soul, like a bird at last set free, reaches the endless space and light and music for which we were created. Thenceforth, I'm convinced, you'll be able to protect me as never before, and to do this you'll have a power of persuasion a million times greater than it is now, though it's very great already. You'll have the power you've most wanted to have, the magic power of bringing happiness. How grateful I am to dear Sister Valcourt for her kind consideration of us, for her thinking, for instance, of bringing you to the telephone yesterday so you could talk to me. Grateful to Sister Rose as well, who tends you with such good care.

I found the beautiful prayer by Teilhard de Chardin that I like so much. Here it is:

> Let me recognize you, Lord,
> in each power that seems
> bent on my destruction,
> the wear and tear of age,
> the pain that makes me small;
> in all these hours of darkness,
> let me understand, O God, that
> this is you at work, sadly
> parting the fibres of my being,
> drawing me away to you.

All my thoughts from dawn to dusk are for you, and even in my dreams at night. You constantly occupy my mind. It's not possible to be closer to someone than I am to you at every moment, through the unrelenting power of my will and the love in my heart.

Marcel thinks of you almost constantly as well. He loves you like a very dear sister who is very, very close to him. We're on either side of you, each holding one of your hands in ours.

The fondest love in all the world,

Gabrielle

Quebec City, April 21, 1970

Ma chère Bernadette,
Another of your letter-cards arrived yesterday to reassure and delight me. Your pen is as generous as your heart. In fact, how many, many letters you've written in your life, always loving and always composed so as to lift one's spirits, dejected spirits at times.

The Madeleines have told me they also have had a note from you, and they're as proud of it as of a treasure to be kept for ever.

Spring, which I thought had come to stay, is lying low this morning, giving way to a wet and gloomy day. But never mind, when we wait for the sun we're all the happier to see it eventually. Still, I'm impatient to hear the snow geese one of these fine mornings, great flights of them high in the sky, returning after spending the winter like millionaires on southern shores. Their noisy chatter up there in the sky as they pass over the city is strange and wonderful to hear through the calm of a morning. What are they saying? Are they agreeing on the route to follow, where to stop, and their destination? Or are they trying to make themselves understood by us on earth, saying perhaps, "Hey, we're back, friends on earth down there, we're back!" And we down here are happy just to know that the great, free birds are really back.

I've said before and I firmly believe that the human soul is much like a bird that keeps seeking total freedom. Perhaps it's because of this special affinity that the soul is so moved to hear the cry of the geese in their migrating flights overhead.

My dear little sister, did you sleep better last night? Were you able to get some rest? There's nothing in the world I wish more for you these days. At all times I think of myself as being close to you. At all times I'm holding your hand in mine. Distance can't change this in the least. Through the full strength of my will I'm staying at your side. Your lovely letters, Sister Valcourt's, our little talks on the telephone, another talk I had with Antonia, all this helps me picture you from morning till night, to refresh the beautiful memories I brought back from Manitoba and will always have. So my imagination can follow you all day long, and never really leaves you.

Think about this: do you know anyone who's better loved than you? Those telephone calls from the far corners of this huge country, the telegrams, the letters coming as thick as rain, the fervent prayers all around you, the ardent affection people have for you . . . what more, what further proof do you need to be convinced that you're loved as few ever are? But it's right and proper that people should love you so, for they are only giving you back what you've given to others in armfuls. You confessed to me one day that your long, long years of teaching seemed confining in a way, and it may be true, and if so the freedom you gave up for it was immeasurable, but what you yourself perhaps don't see is the wealth that one generation of children after another owes to you for the best of yourself, given unflaggingly. You are the rich earth that has given birth to roses, carnations, flowers of all kinds, in profusion and variety that you can't even imagine. But they are testimony to you even so. They are "The host of golden daffodils . . . dancing in the sun."

Sleep now if you can, dear sister, if all this chatter hasn't stirred you up too much. Sleep in trust, your little hand in mine, your heart in repose.

My deepest, fondest love,

Gabrielle

Quebec City, April 22, 1970

Ma chère Dédette,

I'm still going to mass every day for you, and for myself find comfort in this, but alas, I don't seem to be obtaining what I've been asking for you, that your pain be calmed. Sister Rose Desrochers has written me a touching letter in which she tells me that you're in quite intense pain. How it hurts to hear this! But in my prayers yesterday at five o'clock mass I called upon our little mother for help, and she's never yet failed me when I've called on her this way. She'll surely come to your aid because she's capable of anything to help her children. Berthe Simard, whom I telephoned on Monday, told me she had received a letter from you and was moved beyond expression. Dear angel, ill as you are you manage to keep up a flood of correspondence, still sending your little messages of love to the four corners of the country, all bearing the mark of your ardent soul. All who receive them are overjoyed, and the burdens in their lives are lifted for a moment. Such is your power and you'll never lose it, for the riches of the soul, amassed with toil and effort throughout a life, cannot be lost. These are the only powers that will never be taken from us.

Our cold, gloomy weather continues, and I long for the tall sky filled with light that I saw from your room on some days. I miss you very much. Those visits I had with you every day were a great joy to me and I shall always treasure their memory. I would so love to be with you, doing those little things for you that I had such pleasure doing. The truth is that in my heart I'm still there beside you, through all the power of my will and imagination, as I wrote you yesterday. Still, I envy Antonia, for example, who can visit you in person. She is another who is deeply fond of you. How is it that you've made so many people fond of you? There's magic in this, just as there's magic in all our loving, and most of all perhaps in our love of the divine, and in the mysterious divine love that envelops the universe. The other day it dawned on me that we love life as we do because life is God, a part of God, a part of God which is more or less tangible, whereas the other part, which is immense, is out of view beyond the horizon. And in order to know God we must love life as you love it. Loving life is the most important, the most essential of all prayers.

Here's another thought about this from the Hindu religion:

Certain is death for all yet to be born.
And certain is birth for all who die.

I'm staying beside you, keeping your hand in mine. The little child in the photograph has become your protector, and is staying near you to defend you and give you help.

My love to you,

Gabrielle

Don't tire yourself replying for the moment. Just answer through a little prayer from the bottom of your heart.

Quebec City, April 23, 1970

Ma chère Dédette,
It's two weeks yesterday since I left you, but I'd become so accustomed to the sweet pleasure of my visits with you and the joy they brought me that it seems like a century. If there hadn't been obligations requiring me to be here, which couldn't wait, I would have stayed with you longer, and how happy it would have made me! If the weather improves (it's foggy just now) I may go with a friend for a short drive that will take us through Sainte-Anne-de-Beaupré. I'll stop and say a little prayer for you in the basilica if we go. If not, I'll say it in Saint Dominique Church next door, as I do every day.

Spring is having trouble getting started, but it's true that in general it comes later here than in Manitoba. What enchants me most out there is the sky, as I've said a hundred times already. To find one bigger and bluer you have to go to Greece. There's reason for the sky being almost constantly present in all the works of Homer, the greatest of Greek writers. Everywhere in both the Iliad and the Odyssey, on almost every page, there are references to "the light of the sky". We should take the expression literally, but also figuratively I think, for on that day when the end comes, the wondrous light we'll see, by which I imagine we'll be transfigured, can only come from the sky. Perhaps it's already near, much nearer than we think, on the other side of some dark and ordinary-looking promontory of rock which is just enough to block our view of a vast and infinite landscape of dazzling colour and beauty. If today I were to rewrite my little story about Dédette arriving in Paradise[132], I'd do it very differently, because in those days I was a childish little ninny who didn't understand much about the human heart. If I had it to do over, instead of a convent to receive Dédette I'd make it a prairie bathed in sunlight and dotted with the prettiest flowers that ever were, and smelling sweet with fragrant grasses and a cool breeze, and livened by the murmur of a running brook. In the distance there would be a line of graceful young birches with shimmering leaves, and behind them their father-trees, old birches whose bark you can pull off without damaging the trees, for making pretty calendars, all showing the same glorious date forever more. That's what I'd say if I were rewriting this story, and I'd probably include some birds too, and a friendly roof somewhere in the scene. Then I'd have you reunited with Clémence. And others would come — Antonia, Sister Valcourt, Sister Rose, Berthe Simard, our little mother, people from today and yesterday, and we'd all get along famously together.

You're going to tell me that this is as crazy as the first story. But perhaps it isn't. I have a feeling it's closer to the truth.

Now here I am still beside you, holding your dear little hand in mine, with all my thoughts for you, praying with all my heart for your peace and comfort. Try to sleep now.

Much love to you,

Gabrielle

You too, say a prayer for me — I need it badly.

Quebec City, April 24, 1970

Ma chère petite Dédette,

I'm beside you, closer than ever, holding your hands tight in mine, my heart heavy and aching because you're in pain, yet consoled by the thought that God can hear our prayers and will come to your rescue. I've just come from the quarter-to-five mass, where once again I took communion for you. My dear little sister, you can do so much for me, even stricken with illness as you are, for however things may seem, I have a feeling your prayers are more powerful and influential than ever. I'm sure you can gain me the courage to live first of all, and then a marvellous shower of blessings. Just as you have put yourself in my hands in a sense since you've been ill, I'm putting myself in yours so you'll take care of me and never leave me alone.

All my love to you. Did you get the photographs? Dear child, how I would love to have seen the smile those pictures must have brought to your face!

My love once again,

Gabrielle

Quebec City, April 25, 1970

Ma Dédette, ma très chère soeur,
I don't live two minutes of the day without worrying about you, without praying for your pain to ease, or hoping with all my heart that God will show his infinite love for you, a love I'm as certain of as I am of existing. If I waken during the night, my thoughts, however vague, go straight to you. In the freedom of my imagination, we carry on a steady conversation, you and I. But I would give anything in the world to be near you in reality. You have been a great blessing for me, you know, much more than you might think. First in teaching me patience. Then, with your generous way of perceiving things, increasing my power of perception. Thanks to you, I can see the beauty of the world even more clearly than before. You also teach me generosity, unselfishness, and thoughtfulness of others. And what really counts is that you teach me these things not with words, which fade without much trace, but through example, which cannot be erased. Today the weather is wavering between dull and sunny, between dismal and radiant — rather the way our lives are, somewhere between tears and laughter, between fear and confidence, yet when the final end comes, summer will reign. I'm staying beside you, not moving an inch away, staying as close as I can be, still the "Petite Misère"[133] in the photograph of the two of us as children, when you used to protect me.

My love to you with all my heart,

Gabrielle

Quebec City, April 26, 1970

Ma très chère Dédette,
I called the infirmary this morning to ask how you were and to send loving thoughts from Marcel and me through Sister Rose and Sister Berthe Valcourt. They told me your pain was intense and my heart felt torn in two. At mass again today I'm going to pray with all my soul for the pain to cease and the peace of the Lord to enfold you. My poor dear little sister, I would give all I have for you to be well and happy. God is making you wait for some reason that escapes us, but perhaps one day we shall understand it all. Then we shall all be joyful. I'm so sorry you haven't yet received the photographs I sent you; it's probably because of the postal strike. But I want you at least to know that my love for you deepens from day to day.

A big hug and kiss,

Gabrielle

Quebec City, April 27, 1970

Ma très chère Dédette,
I wished and hoped so hard for you to have a good night last night, when I went to bed and each time I wakened during the night — did I at least obtain this wish?

Listen to this, dear child: everything in life is in motion leading back to its source. I gleaned this thought for you yesterday from a television program discussing the philosophy and mysticism of India. Basically, all the great religions are alike. They all have a common goal. And everything in life is certainly in motion leading back to its source, meaning to something greater and better than it has ever known. Streams go to a river, the river to the sea, the sea, by evaporation, to the great clouds floating in the sky, and we creatures who are made to love and be loved go finally to the never-ending love that we have hungered for all our lives. This is the law of all that lives, and even a tiny animal creature needs to be loved. How much greater must be our need therefore, we who are loving and have the gift of glimpsing and hoping for infinity!

Don't worry about Clémence. I'll see that she has everything she needs. Antonia will help me. And I believe that you too will never abandon her.

I still miss you very much. When I remember all those moments filled with gaiety in spite of all your pain, I'm torn between laughter and tears, as I was then. Of all the pictures I have of you in my head — I have hundreds; my head is an album filled with pictures of my Dédette — I don't think there are any I like better than the one where I see you with your hands on your stomach, laughing in little bursts to spare your incision. And the reason I like this picture of you so much is probably because it's the truest, the one that really says, This is Dédette, now and for ever: laughing, courageous, enchanted with life, someone who keeps growing, striving towards the light even in the darkest hours.

Please, my Dédette, a little prayer again today for me, for Marcel, for those I love.

My deepest love to you,

Gabrielle

Quebec City, April 28, 1970

Ma très chère Bernadette,
If only my letters are reaching you! With this partial postal strike I can't be sure, and it devastates me to think this lifeline between us could be cut. You still haven't received the photos I sent off to you in such haste. If my letters are in fact delayed, you mustn't think I've stopped being with you from morning till night, almost from night till morning as well, for if I wake during the night I think at once of you.

I haven't stopped going to mass and taking communion for you every day, either. I'm not praying for anything in particular any more. I just sit in the house of God and let my heart breathe its lament and give itself over to him. What else can we do? After a while I feel calmer, and daydream about all of us being at peace one day — and try to imagine what it will be like, unsuccessfully of course. Still, I feel I'm close to touching the invisible and the answer is there, very near and wonderful.

And I always end up thinking that you're the one who is going to bring me the courage to live, and the patience, and perhaps even joy again, though at the moment it doesn't seem possible that I'll ever know joy again. Anyway, if I do it will be because of you, because once again you have shown me the way.

. . . Shown the way with all manner of small signs — this is what you're going to do, you'll see; you're going to arrange to show us the way and make it easier for us. And what is more, I think your memory will always sing in the gentle breeze of summer, you'll be forever present on the broad horizon of the river, and I shall always hear your dear voice mingled with the rustle of birch leaves and the murmur of the rising tide. And then your happiness will be unbounded, since you'll be part of everything that speaks to us of happiness on earth. How our Eternal Father must cherish you! The works that he created in order to make us love this earth, you have loved so much! He must say to himself, "This child, this Bernadette, of all that is delightful, marvellous, enchanting, nothing is lost on her. She has seen and loved it all. She has prepared herself fittingly for eternity, adoring what I have made, adoring life. Who loves me," the Saviour must say, "who has not passionately loved life and the beauty of the world?"

He must also say, "She has made many and precious friends, this Bernadette. See all the letters coming to her from East and West, through the sky like birds, through strikes here and bad weather there, arriving in spite of all. See the flowers, the telephone calls, the messages of loving friendship from all parts. This is how I like to see my children, taken up with loving one another. And my Bernadette has done what is most important: she has taught others to love. As her reward I will grant that she may favour those she loved on earth with special care, unending care forever more."

What do you think of my story, Dédette my dear? Is it crazy? No, it's wise and true, isn't it?

I'm staying beside you. I'm fluffing up your pillow. I'm holding your hand. And I'm praying with you, trying to trust like a child.

Good night sweet Prince. . .
May a flight of angels sing thee to thy rest. . . .

My love to you. Marcel's also.

Gabrielle

Quebec City, April 29, 1970

Ma très chère Dédette,
I don't know if this letter will reach you. It's been announced that mailboxes may not be cleared today and perhaps not for several days. I must take this letter to the central post office if it's to have a chance of leaving today. I'll do it gladly because above all I want to keep this link with you intact.

I thought of you a great deal yesterday at mass. With intense concentration. I truly saw you before me — or inside me, rather. I was talking to you as I've been doing for several weeks. I thought I sensed concern over Clémence weighing on you and I told you to stop worrying, that for the time being Antonia would make sure Clémence was all right, and for later I would think about what should be done. Also that God would certainly keep protecting her as he has always done before. In fact, she has been like the birds and the lilies of the fields, neither spinning nor weaving, yet she has lacked nothing. If you want, I'll do as you told me you'd like one day when I was with you in Saint-Boniface, and bring Clémence and Antonia to Petite-Rivière, whether you can come with them or not. Though of course you'll be there with us anyway, whatever happens. Besides, you won't ever fail me. This is what you told me on the telephone the last time we spoke. This is what you've written me too, and I must believe it, I absolutely must. You will be my courage, you will be my light, you will be my patience. You have suffered quite enough to have earned this much.

As I was saying, yesterday at mass I was thinking of you with phenomenal concentration. I was grieving over you through no fault of yours. I was grieving because you're in such pain. My grief seemed to me incurable, appalling; I couldn't accept it, as they say, and yet — how can I put it? — cruel though it was, it was not destroying me the way thwarted ambition or wounded self-esteem can do. On the contrary, it seemed to me that such extreme grief was of a kind that breaks down the walls around one's soul, which is invariably rather self-absorbed, rather wrapped up in itself, and was forcing me to grow in spite of myself. I don't think we grow in any other way. As Maman used to say — she was a great philosopher in her way — life makes us grow in spite of ourselves.

Then I saw that you had grown so much I'm still amazed. Gradually the grief I mentioned calmed. Through the mysterious law of mutual help between souls, I received strength from you, who have none left. And perhaps at that moment you received some from me, and I had none left to give either.

Let's keep praying for one another in the same selfless spirit, and God will surely be pleased.

My dear little Bernadette, here I am with you again — can't you see me? — standing beside you, my hand on your brow, smiling at you, for when all is said and done, why should we be anxious and sad? Because everything goes to the sea . . . everything goes to the absolute . . . everything goes to unending bliss. . . .

If I ever write another book, believe me, my Bernadette, it will largely be owing to what you have wrought in me. It will be the work of a soul cleansed by your example. And you will whisper to me what must be said to humankind about suffering, about separation, and about our reunion and homecoming in love triumphant[134].

Be calm, dear child, and have confidence.

Lovingly,

Gabrielle

Quebec City, April 30, 1970

Ma très chère Bernadette,
Yesterday I received the little box full of letters of mine that you've been keeping all this time. I've read a few and discovered something I knew, though not well enough, and that is how much I have loved you, how much I still love you. Bonds of exceptional tenderness have grown between us through the years, this is clear. When I saw these letters a lump came to my throat, with grief and also a kind of joy, for they were bringing me proof of these bonds of tenderness. I wept as I read two or three. If at times I've fairly successfully conveyed the profound feeling I've always had for you, which has deepened through the years, if I've expressed this love in my heart for you reasonably well at times, it's still nothing compared to what I really feel. Words are never powerful enough to express our feelings, or anything that has to do with the soul. Yet all my life I have kept trying to find words to express this turmoil, this perpetual stirring, this inner life of our being.

Dear, dear Bernadette, it's a beautiful day today. A day that promises to be a perfect day of spring. I even think I see signs of renewed life at the tips of the branches of the trees I can see from my window. And at this I'm overjoyed and sad at the same time. These days my heart swings back and forth between the two poles of our lives, joy and pain, darkness and light, rain and sunshine. I've told you before, and it's true, that if I ever really feel joy again it will be your doing, it will be because you have obtained this greatest of all gifts for me, the true breath of God on me, his hand on my frail shoulder in simple tenderness. Perhaps it will be like a great coffer that fills up again the minute we dip into it. Or like the immensity of the sea. But once again you must agree that our words are inadequate to translate the great emotions that stir our souls and the mysterious certainties deep in our hearts. Yet these inexpressible certainties are the greatest truths in our lives, and our most reliable guides. God speaks to us through small signs that can escape us if we're always preoccupied with what we're doing, always restless, scurrying from pillar to post. I think no one has understood these small signs better than you, these signs that God has sent us in the language of the wind, flowers, fluttering leaves, in the smile of a child, the light of the sky, the vastness of the waters of the Lake.

God must be thinking, although I did not create the Lake for

Bernadette alone, it would have been worth my while, for who has seen it better than she, has listened to it more intently, has spoken more of it, and who, in her letters each summer, has better helped others to know its freshness, vastness, and eternal whispering?

No one in fact has been happier than my Bernadette beside my great Manitoba lake. No one has deserved more to have it always and for ever, and I have given it specially to her because it has always been "her" lake.

I'm comforted now, "my child, my sister", because I see you sitting on the sand beside this eternally cool, changing water, your coif stirred just barely by a slight breeze, your nostrils almost quivering, your face in repose, all signs of illness erased, a smile on your lips and joy in your heart, my dearest Dédette.

Lovingly,

Gabrielle

May 1970

Quebec City, May 1, 1970

Ma chère Dédette,

Today is the first day of May. It reminds me of my days as a teacher in Saint-Boniface, when I was teaching my little pupils the song "Today's the first of May, the merry month of May. . . ." I remember it so well because I'd taken months to learn it myself, having so little ear and so much trouble holding a tune. Anyway, this was one tune I did learn and can still hear in my head. And it (the song) reminds me of the round the children used to dance as they sang the song. It's a sweet and precious memory.

Yesterday evening Antonia, who had Clémence visiting, was kind enough to call me on the telephone so I could talk to them both. Telephone conversations with Clémence don't go very far. Either she doesn't hear well or she only thinks about whatever interests her at the time; she just keeps talking and pays no attention to what you're asking her. But she feels comfortable with Antonia and seemed pleased to be there; she told me all about some little things she intends to buy at Eaton's with Antonia's help. I suspect you've had a hand in this plan, you're always so anxious to protect Clémence, to take care of her. Don't worry about her though. I'm convinced there will always be someone to help her and love her.

I'm continuing my earnest prayers for you, and for me. I'm always at your side, every minute that goes by. I'm staying near you. I'm wishing with all my heart for your pain to disappear.

My fondest love,

Gabrielle

Quebec City, May 2, 1970

Ma très chère Dédette,

I can't let a day pass without writing at least a few lines to you, so today I'm doing it in haste, at seven in the morning, before leaving for Petite-Rivière. Marcel insists on running up to look at his roses in daylight, having covered them with piles of dead branches and earth last autumn to protect them from the frost. Sadly, for all our precautions, we'll probably find many of our perennials dead, because the cold was severe last winter in a period when there was too little snow on the ground to provide them with a comforter. We always have to expect a few of our plants to die each year, but every time it happens it makes us sad. We won't have fine weather for our little trip; we should have gone yesterday, which had all the makings of a real summer's day. It's drizzling at present and the wind is howling. Never mind, while Marcel attends to his plants I'll stay indoors at Berthe's. And we'll talk about you. Who else would we talk about, we two, when we love you so? I knew you'd had a visit from Fernand and Léontine and this cheered me up a little, as I imagine it did you. But I imagine too that having visitors must be more and more tiring for you; you've always been so inclined to give of yourself, to outdo yourself really "receiving" visitors. I wish all the more that I were with you still, attending to your needs, anticipating your wants. I keep praying that God will show you his love, his kindness. All I am these days is a single thought, which is you, my best of sisters, my Dédette. Please don't you abandon me, either. Keep me in your heart, in your soul. Only on this condition shall I have strength. And God grant that I manage to communicate some of it to you across the miles through my love for you, which has always been great but all of a sudden has begun growing prodigiously, as if from a beneficial rain or intensive care. This is one plant at least that the frost won't touch.

Yesterday I received a note from our faithful Sister Rose, telling me that she and Sister Monique have finally received the books I put in the mail for them two weeks ago. I hope very much that in the same delivery the postman also brought you those big photographs, and that they'll bring delight to your eyes . . . your magnificent grey eyes, cloud grey, faraway grey, misty-the-way-it-is-today grey, dear eyes that have shone with joy at the humblest gift from heaven to our earth, and have reflected the infinite love of God. These dear eyes may see the light that clarifies all, explains all, embraces all before mine do. If so, please try to send me a ray of this light. You'll send it down from heaven to earth like a little silken ladder, a fragile one no doubt, on which I'll get a footing, now and then managing to climb a few of its woven rungs, blown by the wind, swinging in the void, but steadied by your voice and counsel.

One day we shall at last be together again, and we shall at last recognize and be reunited with others we love.

Sleep now, my Bernadette, sleep peacefully, as trusting children sleep, for life is made by love and for love.

Ever so fondly,

Gabrielle

Quebec City, May 3, 1970

Ma chère, chère Dédette,

We went to Petite-Rivière-Saint-François yesterday, and I thought about you all the way there, all the way back, and almost all the time we were there. The frost did less damage to our plants than we'd expected. The crocuses were already up and opening their funny little white flowers. It was an odd day, partly angry and partly radiant. Now and then it rained briefly, though the sun was still shining. The effect was curious. It was a day that made me think of a child laughing through its tears. Will the hand of God soon cure us both of our sorrow? Will joy be reigning in us soon? At this moment I have difficulty believing so, yet blind conviction tells me that our great hope of triumph cannot fail us.

Berthe and I had a quiet conversation in her kitchen, talking about you, recalling a great many memories of the happy times we all had together. Once in a while I would look through the big bay window Berthe has had made to replace the little, old-fashioned windows that used to be there, out to the river which yesterday was grey like your eyes and covered with wonderful little white, scurrying waves. It's the south wind ruffling the water that makes these bubbling crests which look so pretty from shore. Yesterday I saw all these things through you, through your eyes, through your love for them, and they were more beautiful than ever before, though they made my heart ache terribly. I missed mass for you for the first time in three weeks. Still, contemplating the river and sky was a substitute for prayer yesterday, perhaps. Don't you think so? Besides, I'll be at mass today and I'll pray even harder for you, if that's possible.

You should have heard the wind in our pine trees, grown tall and beautiful by now. The wind is at its most melodious in pine trees and I've long wondered why. Perhaps it's because of the fine foliage. There are thousands of tiny spaces for the wind to pass through and make the needles sing. I really know nothing about this, but I've always been enchanted with the sound of the south wind in the pines. I imagine I'm hearing a hymn of praise for the liberation of souls. Yours and mine may one day rise together in this same little clump of pines, joining the chorus of joy in deliverance. I have no ear at all but perhaps at long last I'll sing on key.

My fondest, tenderest love to you, my dear Dédette,

Gabrielle

P.S. My thanks to Sister Rose for the note I received from her yesterday. Thanks to her also for taking such good care of you. My very kindest regards to Sister Valcourt.

Quebec City, May 4, 1970

Ma très chère Bernadette,

I thought about you just about every second of the day yesterday, and rose this morning still thinking of you. My grief is extreme not to be at your side, trying to help you. It's a beautiful day today, but my heart remains bleak. I'd like you to forgive me for the wrongs I may have done you, the love and generosity I failed to show you at certain times when I was young, a kind of selfishness. Forgive me these things. On your side I see nothing, not a thing I could reproach you for. I've thought and thought but my memories contain nothing whatever to your discredit.

They are all happy memories, beautiful memories, all the most pleasant evidence imaginable in your favour. Pure, sweet memories, like beautiful white birds of the seashore. They are among the most precious memories of my life. I don't remember a single letter from you, for example, that hasn't brought me comfort, that hasn't soothed me like a balm. I'm asking Our Lord God to take account of these lovely letters you've written me, your countless gestures of love, and if he considers just the help that I alone have received from you, this in itself is an immensely powerful plea. But he knows this, of course, and doesn't need to be reminded of all the love you've shown me. I need only reread your letters, where it shines. I need only remember your face, your eyes, where it shone each time I came to see you in the hospital, and later the infirmary.

Today I'll be at mass again for you. I'll never leave your side, and please, I beg you, don't ever leave mine. Say thank you to Sister Superior[135], who is so good to us. Her kind concern for Clémence, for Adèle also, is really what comforts me most at present.

My love to you, and remember, I'm with you night and day.

Gabrielle

Quebec City, [May 5,] 1970[136]

Ma très chère Bernadette,

I'm desperately sad to think that a twenty-four-hour strike of postal employees in Quebec City prevented my letter of yesterday from leaving when it should have, and that consequently you'll have had a day without any letter from me. To think of this, when I'm in such a hurry to sit down and write you as soon as I'm up every morning, because my first thoughts the minute I wake are of you! I've been fit to be tied over this strike, but what can we do about it? If only this letter, at least, reaches you to bring you all my love.

Did I write you or tell you that Marcel is taking pottery lessons? He's begun to bring home some quite nicely turned pieces. Most important, it does him good and relaxes the nervous tension that troubles so many men nowadays — and women too. Yesterday at mass I prayed for you very, very hard, Dédette mine. I keep asking that you'll be delivered from your suffering. The thought that you're in such pain is really more than I can bear. I received a kind letter yesterday from Sister Berthe. She tells me that she reads my letters aloud to you. I rather suspected as much. Far from being embarrassed, I think I'm delighted, because it means all three of us have suffered together and this makes us a very close little threesome, united by deep affection, and wonderfully in harmony.

But who would have thought that thanks to you, Sister Berthe and I would become friends through being so strongly allied for your protection?

I promise I'll write you a longer letter tomorrow, Dédette my dear.

Much love,

Gabrielle

Quebec City, May 6, 1970

Ma chère Dédette,

A thousand thanks to our sweet friend Sister Berthe, who so very kindly called me on the telephone yesterday to give me your news. I would have loved to hear your dear voice at the end of the line, but I know that this is now more than you have strength for. In fact, dear sister, you've done more than you have strength for all your life, borne along by the bravest of spirits. Your spirit, today betrayed by your poor pain-filled body, is on the eve — do you hear me? — on the eve of rediscovering its extraordinary vigour, its joy, its passion for God's creation, all that has made us love our Dédette as much as we do. She is on the eve of taking flight in total freedom, a poor bird that has suffered in captivity, however beautiful life may be, for life is still at best a kind of cage, is it not? Everything we love most about life, seeing the sky in all its depth, the prairies to infinity, immense reaches of water, long rivers flowing towards the sea, all the things we love most in life — think carefully about this — are precisely those that make us forget our captivity and dream of an absolute. They are the things that hint of limitless space, and have spoken to us of eternity every day of our lives; the things that have given our dream a taste of eternity. Our moments of joy are moments plucked from the mystery of eternity. I have always believed that we come closest to creation's supreme truth in our moments of elation. Trust the joy which so many, many times has come to inhabit you. This is what speaks the truth, my Dédette; it is this that never deceives us, that leads us to the Lord, and awaits us. A radiant joy just like a blissful summer day beside great Lake Winnipeg. The infinite joy that sometimes shows in a human face. The joy in a human heart hearing a call to God through the wondrous marvels of creation. This is the joy you will know, my Dédette, believe me; there are only a few steps on the dark side still to go. I will help you walk these difficult steps. I will hold your hand. And then I shall be infinitely envious because you will be arriving beyond the darkness before me, in the marvellous fullness of the world's ultimate reality revealed at last. I'll envy you being born into true life; you glowing like a butterfly freshly emerged from the chrysalis; you shimmering in God's light like birch leaves in the wind and sun. And you will come and console me when I'm depressed, speak to me softly of hope beyond doubt, and faith in beauty. And ever after I shall see you among your beloved birches, with their melodious rustling and the grace of their whiteness.

Oh yes, my Dédette, trust in joy and beauty, our surest guides, the infallible star in our lives.

All my love to you,

Gabrielle

Quebec City, May 7, 1970

Ma très chère Bernadette,
I dreamed last night that we were beside a great expanse of clear water in the sun. We were about to leave the shore, setting off on a voyage whose end we could not know, but the sea was so beautiful and the sky so benign that we were certain this voyage was going to be the best of voyages. In my dream we were full of gaiety and hope. When I woke I wondered if I shouldn't take this dream as a glimpse of the bliss that is hidden from us during this life, but towards which we keep walking from the time of our birth. In any case, this strange dream has comforted me, you might say. Though my heart was heavy when I fell asleep, I awoke less sad than usual. If you come to know this eternal bliss before I do — this joy revealed to us only beyond a bend — please, my Dédette, find a way to let me know how it will be, a way to give me a glimpse of the soul's prodigious wonder on passing through those wide-open gates into the brilliance and splendour of eternity.

Meanwhile don't be afraid. Lean on me as you did when we used to walk the main hallway of the convent together — ah, cherished memory that will last as long as I live! Then you will need only a few steps more in the shadows before you emerge into total daylight, total companionship, and a rapture for which your rapture beside the lake was merely a prelude. Now your great Lake Winnipeg will sough and glitter in the sun all the time.

You yearned for freedom as you did these last years because you had given yours to God in sacrifice when you were very young, hadn't looked before you leapt, so to speak. You gave what you most loved, your precious freedom, and because your sacrifice was immense, the ecstasy of your reward, your freedom restored, will also be boundless.

One day when I was with you in the hospital, you told me about a certain summer day when you were a child, and the ecstasy you felt to be living that day. Why would such memories last a lifetime if they contained no truth, if they were not instants from eternity, brief glimpses of God himself?

All my love to you, dear, dear Dédette,

Gabrielle

Quebec City, May 10, 1970

Ma chère Bernadette,
Yesterday evening I had the pleasure of speaking on the telephone to Sister Rose and then Sister Berthe, and heard that you've taken to eating popsicles. You must be a comical sight lying in bed sucking popsicles! But I'm glad, so very glad, if you can digest those at least. Yesterday I didn't budge from the house. I was rather tired and Marcel went by himself to Petite-Rivière to plant a dozen nasturtium plants and as many anemones — far too early in my opinion. Sixty-five miles of driving, double that to go and come back, just to plant his little growing things is a bit much, don't you think? But it was a lovely day and Marcel was dying to get his hands into some earth. It takes hold of him every spring like a sickness and there's no resisting it. And after all the effort we'll have a tangled, dishevelled, and rather higgledy-piggledy garden, like the one a certain Frenchman had long ago in Saint-Boniface; he lived in a kind of shack beyond a jumble of flowers the like of which I've never seen anywhere else, do you remember the place? I'd be hard put to say what street the eccentric old fellow lived on, but I still have a picture in my mind of that handkerchief-sized garden with hundreds and hundreds of flowers, all on top of each other. Maman used to send me there sometimes, I'm not sure it wasn't to pick up laundry the old man had washed, and I'd stay at the gate for hours looking at this unbelievable little garden that made me think of a patchwork quilt. In the end my head would be spinning the way it often does today at exhibitions of modern art. I dreamed of you again last night, a pleasant dream I think, since it left me with a pleasant feeling, but I've forgotten the details. They evaporated as soon as I woke, like a morning mist with the first rays of sunshine.

I have some news that's going to please you: I'm about to sign an agreement with the National Film Board, which is going to make a short film based on *Where Nests the Water Hen*, in English and French, for Manitoba's centennial celebrations[137]. It will just be a little film with pictures and some narration I suppose, and I don't know yet how good it will be, but let's hope it will be well done.

Sister Berthe, our treasured friend, told me yesterday that you were a little calmer. Are you sleeping a bit better for it? How happy I'd be if I suddenly learned you'd been relieved of your pain! The good Lord must be tired of hearing me ask for the same thing all the time.

All our friends keep asking after you and send you their warmest regards. Marcel too.

Lovingly,

Gabrielle

Quebec City, May 11, 1970

Ma chère Dédette,

I'm just out of bed and am writing a quick word to catch the mail, which will be leaving soon. It's a grey, drizzly day, but it's doing a lot of good to the vegetation. The year's young leaves are just out. From here I can see their tender greenery on the topmost branches of trees grown as high as my windows. I'm sorry you have no view of even a single tree from your room. But we have everything inside us if we only know how to find it. Just close your eyes and order up the most beautiful tree you've ever seen, and there it will be to your inner eye. True possession of things is here, not in our hands but in our souls, which alone can preserve the things we love.

A thousand thanks each passing day to Sister Rose for tending you with such devotion, to Sister Berthe for lavishing such love on you, to you as well, my dear Dédette, for being what you are, a little sister who has no equal when it comes to being lovable. Where did she learn to be so lovable? It must be her special secret. She does it very well anyway, and all by herself can gather more friendship and affection in a single day than some poor folk in a whole year. May God hold her to his heart, his favourite child.

My fondest love,

Gabrielle

Quebec City, May 11, 1970

Ma chère Dédette à moi,
The postal strike may begin again so I'm writing you a second time today. Let's say this second letter of the same date will count for tomorrow. It would really hurt me if you didn't receive a word from me every day to show that I care about you all the time and love you deeply. I told you it was a rather gloomy day. The wind is wailing over the rooftops. Yet these rather dark, damp days are good for everything that grows. If we could ban them we probably would without a second thought, but we'd be doing a disservice to nature, which we love; nature needs the rest afforded by these days, which to us are graceless and depressing. The thing that's essential for making us grow is something we can't even see. Hence the trust we must place in creation, in the Creator. In a few minutes I'll be going to mass for you. I go every day, pleased to be doing at least this for you. It helps me too, besides. I feel that these moments I spend in church because of you, for you, unite us still more firmly than ever before. The other day, as if he were speaking directly to me, the young curate who was saying mass began more or less like this: that sometimes we are sad with a sadness that we feel will never lift, yet it leads us to joy, and is indeed the only path that can lead us to joy.

All my love to you,

Gabrielle

Quebec City, May 12, 1970

Ma chère petite Dédette,
Yesterday during mass I thought about you, and me, and Maman, and everyone in our family, and I thought that, strange though we all are, and though all of us in our own ways have had difficult lives, we have certainly known joy, at least you and I have, and that's rare you know, because not many people ever really know joy. They know pleasure,

minor passing happiness, they have their comforts, their whims gratified, minor satisfactions all their lives, because that's all they ever really look for; they know as little about joy as about the profound distress that can torture a person. But we're privileged souls, we're among those few human beings who have known joy more than once in the course of their existence . . . ten times, twenty times, even a hundred times perhaps. That is a great deal when you consider how millions of unfortunate lives go by without ever even glimpsing joy. Personally, I never stop trying to define it and you may say I'm getting tiresome over this, but I really believe that in joy we are a hair's breadth from the divine. All of a sudden we are lifted by an invisible presence and in this fleeting moment are united with the infinite, of which we are a tiny piece. This is what gives us that feeling of extreme well-being, elation and serenity both at once. This is why I say to you, believe in joy, Dédette mine, it speaks the truth; it cannot deceive us. It is joy that awaits us in the end.

I'm going to mass to pray with all my heart for both of us, and also for Sister Berthe, whom I'm learning to love like another sister whom Heaven has granted me at a time when I have need of one.

My fondest love to you, my Dédette,

Gabrielle

Quebec City, May 13, 1970

Mon enfant, ma soeur, ma Dédette,
The year's new leaves that I talked about yesterday are already half open, coaxed by a little rain last night, and are forming a beautiful backdrop around my bedroom, a tender, silky green, stirring with the wind. But alas, all this young greenery does my sinuses no good; I began to sneeze the minute I woke. I sneeze the way Papa used to, remember? — twenty, thirty times in a row and very noisily, which isn't too elegant, but how can I help it?

My poor dear Dédette, how I wish for an end to your suffering, how

I wish for all the pain you're enduring to leave you at last! I think only of this, I keep praying for this. Though he must have his reasons, God often takes his time to answer us, don't you find?

Yesterday, the day that was so miserable in the morning turned beautiful by evening. So it will surely be with our lives, which beyond doubt will end in beauty. Anyway, yesterday there was a summery feeling in the air and on every side you could hear the birds singing busily. A few days earlier the wild geese winging in flights from the south towards the Arctic came to land not far from Quebec City. This is their resting place, where they pause on their long, exhausting journey and rebuild their strength. They stay here on the shores of the Saint Lawrence River, thousands and thousands of them, feeling safe and at home, fearing nothing; hunting them at this time is forbidden. Sometimes they rise again into the sky and fly over the city — or else it's newcomers arriving — and you can hear their strange, haunting cry, like a call to something better than we have ever known on earth. In any event, it's a cry that seems suddenly to release the knots in one's heart. Looking up to watch the flight of those great, free birds, who hasn't dreamed of being like these fortunate, unfettered creatures slicing through the air, perfectly in their element up there in the sky? Did you know that snow geese — and perhaps Canada geese[138] — marry once and for all and never in their lives change mates, and remain alone if their mates die? Sometimes at the end of a large flight you'll see one or two or three laggards letting themselves get left behind a bit; these are the ones that have lost their mates, and perhaps have never ceased to grieve for them. Don't think I'm making this up. All of it's true and proven.

Dédette mine, I'd so love to send you the beautiful cry of the great geese, as we hear it on spring evenings here when a flight is on its way to the north, the lovely, bewitching cry that lifts one's soul with hope.

I shall go to mass for you again today. Then I'll come back to be with you. I'll be close by your side, as I've promised you. I won't budge from there.

A thousand thanks to Sister Rose and Sister Monique.

A thousand pleasant memories for Sister Berthe.

All my love for you, dear Bernadette, and a hug,

Gabrielle

Quebec City, May 14, 1970

Ma très chère Dédette,
Here are the great wild geese I talked about in yesterday's letter. By happy chance I came upon this very opportune picture in the paper yesterday. So here they are in their place of rest, their temporary refuge, where no harm can come to them; here are the messengers of spring . . . perhaps of eternal spring. Their cry, as they cross the sky over the city at night sometimes, is the most beautiful sound you can hear. A distinguished Swedish writer for whom I have the greatest admiration, Selma Lagerlöf, believed that when she heard the geese calling as they flew above the earth she was hearing them calling to humans, inviting them to set off for the shores of infinity.

Are you suffering a little less pain today, Dédette mine? I wish so much for this, I hope for this with so much heart that surely God will answer me. Pray for me too, Dédette my dear, pray for me too. Let's exchange our thoughts, our prayers, our anxieties — or rather, give your anxieties to me if you still have any, so that I may bear them for you.

My tenderest love — oh, if you only knew how tender!

Gabrielle

Quebec City, May 15, 1970

Chère Dédette à moi,
That postmen's strike is still threatening. Meanwhile I'm trying to write you as often as possible. Sometimes I imagine my letter flying like a bird through or over barriers and obstacles, threading its way here, slipping through there, steering between hazards and finally arriving, pleased to have overcome so many difficulties and be in your hands at last. What wouldn't I do to give you a little pleasure? What wouldn't I do to bring a smile to your face?

It's a perfectly beautiful day today. If it's as fine as this tomorrow we may run up to Petite-Rivière, though the trip there and back in a single day — about 130 miles — always leaves me pretty well exhausted. However, there's compensation for this in the pure air and the view of the river, which has no equal, I think, anywhere in its course. Madeleine Lemieux[139], who has already moved with her husband to their house on Ile-aux-Coudres, was in town yesterday for the day. She took the trouble to telephone me and ask how you were. The other Madeleines ask after you frequently. You have a small circle of faithful, affectionate friends here. They love you with a constancy that touches my heart. You won them for ever with that zest for life radiating from you, which I think goes well with a love of God. As I've probably said many times already, how can we love God if not through life? Deep down, they are one and the same thing: love of God and love of life in all its dimensions, with its sorrow as well as its magic.

The other day I made a simple little bouquet of old leaves, pussy-willows, and dried, pale-coloured grasses, which was lovelier, I think, than a bouquet from some grand florist's. I would have loved to send it to you, but it was so fragile I don't think it would have survived the trip. Imagine that I sent it to you anyway, and that it's there beside you reminding you of the mystery of spring, life reborn, the everlasting renewal of life.

Dédette mine, I miss you terribly; I miss your little infirmary room in the convent where I spent those priceless hours with you; I miss "our" Sister Berthe and "our" Sister Rose. I miss you, so quick of mind and still so humorous, even though you're ill.

My fondest love to you,

Gabrielle

Quebec City, May 18, 1970

Ma petite Dédette très chère,
The day before yesterday they announced on the news that there would be no letter pick-up the following day and I haven't written since. Today I hear that mail is being picked up after all so I'm sending you a line in haste. Oh, my dear Dédette, how I'd hate to have you think for a single moment that I'm no longer beside you. I passed through Sainte-Anne-de-Beaupré yesterday and went into the basilica. I don't much like it, with its gewgaws and showiness, its vulgarity, but still, it's a place where many suffering souls have come, a place where God is accustomed to hearing our pleas from here on earth. I talked to him about you, though he already knows you perfectly and envelops you with his love; I talked to him about you as a sister who would like to help her Dédette. He must have heard me.

I'm holding your hand between my two. I don't feel like saying anything any more; I just want to stay beside you in silence, united with you in our unswerving hope in the eternal light and love.

Your Gabrielle

A most affectionate and grateful thank you to our dear friends Sister Berthe, Sister Rose, Sister Monique, and all the others I imagine around you, ready to answer your every need.

Quebec City, May 19, 1970

Chère Dédette,
Will my letter pass the barriers to reach you, dear heart? If God accepted bargains from us humans, you would long since have been relieved of at least some of your pain, and I would be bearing it in return for all you have done for me. All I can do is go to mass every day, sit in a

corner of the nave, and offer my grief for the pain you're enduring; there's no doubt God sees and hears, but he really does tax our poor patience, doesn't he?

I'm desperately sorry Antonia has had to suspend the visits that she enjoyed so and that you enjoyed too. But don't worry, I'm sure she'll be much better and it's a good thing they found out what was wrong with her. It's a bit my fault that this has happened because I made her promise before I left that she would go and have a thorough medical examination. All the same, God is trying us terribly these days, and from every side at once. One day we shall know the reason for it all, the meaning of trial and suffering . . . and how impatient I am at times to have answers to all these "why's" that trouble us! And oh, how hard I'm wishing for sleep for you, and respite from your pain this very day!

All my love to you, my dear, my dearest Dédette,

Gabrielle

[*Note in Gabrielle Roy's hand on the envelope*: Letter not read to Dédette[140].]

Quebec City, May 20, 1970

Ma chère petite Bernadette,
Here's another letter I'm releasing into the blue like a swallow, in hopes it will foil the traps laid here and there by slowdown strikes. Perhaps God will do me the favour of allowing it to slip through the obstacles and reach you, still vibrating with the deep love in my heart for you, with my constant longing to see you at peace and happy, really happy, Dédette mine. I have one single prayer, one obsession, one thing I care about, and it is this. You are never out of my thoughts. You are constantly there before my eyes. Often, you have been my joy in life. Right now you are my deepest sorrow. One day you will be my joy again, I know, nothing but my joy, rediscovered and more marvellous than ever.

I have written to our poor Rodolphe at last, trying to give him some comfort[141]. It was you who guided my hand, you who gave me the courage I needed. It was you who whispered the words to say. Thank you, my dearest little sister, and thank you for your prayers, whose effect, generosity and glowing tenderness, I can feel across the miles.

My love to you and our dear Sister Berthe also,

Gabrielle

[*Note in Gabrielle Roy's hand on the envelope*: Letter arrived too late, not read to Dédette.]

Quebec City, May 21, 1970

Ma chère petite Dédette,

I'm having a lot of trouble finding new things to write you about; my mind is so full of you I don't notice much around me any more. I've just telephoned the convent to find out how you are. I wasn't able to talk to Sister Berthe, who is in retreat, they tell me, but I heard a great deal about you anyway. I asked them to have you say a prayer for me. Dear angel, your prayers must be beyond price. Mine are probably not worth much, but at least there's no lack of them for you. The danger of a strike has faded, it seems, for a time at any rate, so I don't need to worry about the thread of my letters to you being broken. I received a sweet little letter from Clémence telling me she'd rather go and spend a short while, *une secousse*, to use her expression, at Aunt Anna Landry's[142] than take "your aeroplanes" to come and stay with me. She's probably right, really; the trip would likely upset her routine too much. As you wrote me about a year ago, we'll put our plans in the hands of God; he will do with them what is best for us in the end.

Marcel sends you his most affectionate regards and I my fondest love, dear little sister.

Gabrielle

Clémence is always happy to go back to Somerset, which perhaps brings back some of her happiest and most innocent memories of childhood. The ones all of us may rediscover, lovelier than ever, beyond the horizon.

[*Note in Gabrielle Roy's hand on the envelope*: Letter arrived too late, not read to Dédette.]

Quebec City, May 22, 1970

Ma Dédette si chère,
I've begun to miss you again most terribly, the way I've felt so often since I left you over a month ago. It doesn't get one bit better. Even ill, you were more keen-witted, more perceptive, more loving, more interesting than many people who are able-bodied and in the best of health. I miss my Dédette beyond words, which is why I asked them yesterday on the telephone to tell you about my wanting you to say a little prayer for me. For my part, after mass yesterday evening when everyone had left, I stayed a long while in the peace and quiet of the church, with almost all the lights out, thinking about the two of us, and in the silence after a time a kind of peacefulness came over me, as if I had been given a marvellous assurance that you and I would be going hand in hand together towards a dawn the likes of which we had never seen before. A priceless dawn rising over the ends of the earth and bathing us in hope and light. But then this sweet, beautiful moment passed and I was missing you again. Even to see you for two minutes, time enough to wipe your brow, to hold a cup to your lips, would be better than nothing. Yet I do these things in my imagination; in my imagination I never leave your side. So much so that I'm hardly living in what is called reality. To me, indeed, reality exists far more in our dreams than in the small everyday things that keep us busy day after day — at least, the reality towards which our daily tasks should be leading us.

All my love,

Gabrielle

All roads in dreams lead to reality. Does this not mean to God?

[*Note in Gabrielle Roy's hand on the envelope*: Letter arrived too late, not read to Dédette.]

Quebec City, May 24, 1970

Ma très chère petite Dédette,
I'm just back from high mass where, to the sound of the organ and the voices of the choir, I really didn't think about anything but you. The music calmed me somewhat, and I imagined that you too were at peace. At the end of mass, this is what we ask of God as the greatest of gifts, is it not? Give us peace, we pray. No doubt he'll grant peace to all of us in the end.

It's a beautiful summer day today. The leaves whose birth I watched last week are already full out, and their clusters hide my view of the river. Today I'm strangely homesick for the high, light-filled sky of Manitoba. More than skies elsewhere, I think perhaps it beckons us to the light of eternity, to joy finally triumphant.

I've had another little letter from Clémence this week. Aunt Anna Landry, kind soul, has invited her to spend several weeks with her, and Clémence is delighted. I think perhaps I've told you all this already and am repeating myself. Yesterday I had a lovely visit from Yolande and Jean. They were here for a dinner given for the group of civil servants they were with while Jean was studying in Paris. I kept them for a bite of lunch. The two of them are good-looking, happy, well, and in love with one another. How beautiful it is to see two people so in love! We talked about you for a good half of their visit, with great affection evident on all sides. You are and will always be the radiant centre of our family, a nucleus of purity, vibrancy, and so much warmth. God keep you, Dédette mine. A kiss on your forehead and each cheek. Then I'll stay beside you, still and quiet so as not to tire you.

My memories of you — precious, tender memories — always make me think of Sister Berthe. Beside a picture of the one I always see the other. Two pictures to keep.

My love to you and another kiss,

Gabrielle

[*Note in Gabrielle Roy's hand on the envelope*: Letter arrived after Dédette died.]

Notes

1. When her mother died on June 26, 1943, Gabrielle Roy travelled to Manitoba. She had not lived in the province since her departure for Europe in 1937. However, she had returned briefly to the West in the summer of 1942 to write a series of articles, "Peuples du Canada" ("Peoples of Canada"), published in the *Bulletin des agriculteurs*, November 1942 to May 1943, and republished with modifications in *Fragile Lights of Earth.* During this visit she also wrote several articles that appeared in the daily *Le Canada* ("Laisser passer les jeeps", November 24, 1942; "Regards sur l'Ouest", December 7 and 21, 1942, January 5 and 16, 1943).
2. From her trip to the Gaspé Peninsula, where she would often return on holiday, Gabrielle Roy brought back an article entitled "Une voile dans la nuit", which was published in the *Bulletin des agriculteurs* of May 1944 and republished as "The Gaspé Fishermen — A Sail in the Night" in *Fragile Lights of Earth.*
3. Since the autumn of 1940, Gabrielle Roy had been a freelance reporter for this Montreal monthly, in which she published some major series of social-interest articles.
4. Anna Roy, who was born in 1888, was Gabrielle and Bernadette's eldest sister. After teaching for a number of years, she married Albert Painchaud and had three sons, Fernand (who was born in the same year as Gabrielle Roy), Paul, and Gilles. Beginning in 1939, she and her husband lived at Saint-Vital, not far from Saint-Boniface on River Road, along the Red River, in the attractive house they had built; in the family circle this property was called "La Painchaudière".
5. Clémence Roy, another elder sister to Gabrielle and Bernadette, owing to her dependent condition, lived with her mother until the latter's death. Her sisters took charge of her subsequently, and she lived in a succession of homes. She inspired Gabrielle Roy to write "Alicia", a story in *Street of Riches.*
6. Since her return from Europe in 1939, Gabrielle Roy had been living in Montreal, but was in the habit of spending some of her time in this municipality in the Laurentian Mountains north of the city, not far from the village where her mother was born, Saint-Alphonse-de-Rodriguez. She wrote most of *The Tin Flute* in Rawdon.

7. Adèle Roy was another elder sister to Gabrielle and Bernadette, second eldest after Anna. She too was a schoolteacher. Around 1946 she was living in Tangent, Alberta, which Gabrielle Roy visited during her trip to theWest in 1942 (see note 1). Adèle inspired "To Prevent a Marriage" in *Street of Riches.*
8. The street in Saint-Boniface, Manitoba, where the house that Gabrielle Roy was born in is located. Her father had had the house built in 1905 and her mother continued to live there until about 1937. In 1955, Gabrielle Roy gave its name to her book *Rue Deschambault* (*Street of Riches*), which consists of stories inspired by her childhood and early adulthood.
9. Gabrielle Roy's first book, the novel *Bonheur d'occasion*, was published in Montreal by Editions Pascal in March 1945. It was subsequently published in France, winning the Prix Femina in 1947. Before this event, in April 1947, it was published in New York by Reynald & Hitchcock in a translation by Hannah Josephson entitled *The Tin Flute*; it was chosen as a "Book of the Month" by the Literary Guild of America, became a bestseller, and the film rights were sold to a Hollywood producer. Gabrielle Roy also received the Governor General's Award for Literature, the Lorne Pierce Medal of the Royal Society of Canada, and the Medal of the Académie canadienne-française for this book.
10. Annette and Basil Zarov were Montreal photographers. From 1945 on, they were responsible for most of the formal photographs of Gabrielle Roy. For photographs of this period, see in particular the magazine *Pour vous Madame*, November-December 1947.
11. Gabrielle Roy was visiting her sister Anna at "La Painchaudière" (see note 4).
12. At this time Bernadette was at the Mont Carmel Convent in Kenora on Lake of the Woods, near Ontario's Manitoba border. She taught diction and drama, and even mounted plays she wrote herself. She had been living in Kenora for twenty years, but was shortly to return to Saint-Boniface to teach at the Académie Saint-Joseph.

13. *La Liberté* (*La Liberté et Le Patriote*) is a French newspaper in Saint-Boniface. Although *Bonheur d'occasion* was not awarded the Prix Femina until the autumn of 1947, in view of the novel's success in Montreal and in the United States as *The Tin Flute*, as well as Gabrielle Roy's election to the Royal Society of Canada, the writer's first return in four years to the city of her birth had turned into something of a triumphant homecoming. During this visit Gabrielle Roy met Marcel Carbotte, a young physician; they were married in Saint-Boniface a few months later, at the end of August 1947.
14. Since October 1947, Gabrielle Roy had been in Paris with her husband, who was pursuing his studies as a medical specialist at l'Hôpital Broca. Late that autumn, she had received the Prix Femina for *Bonheur d'occasion*; see "How I Received the Femina" ("Comment j'ai reçu le Femina"), an article published in 1956 and republished in *Fragile Lights of Earth.*
15. At this time Bernadette was at the Saint-Jean-Baptiste Convent in Saint-Jean-Baptiste, Manitoba.
16. Lucille Roy — the daughter of Germain, Gabrielle Roy's youngest brother (see note 44) — was about to begin the study of medicine.
17. This was Jeanne Lapointe, a teacher of literature at l'Université Laval in Quebec City.
18. Yolande Roy, the younger sister of Lucille (see note 16), was then seven years old.
19. When they first arrived in Paris, Gabrielle Roy and her husband lived at the Hôtel Lutetia on the Boulevard Raspail. At the time of this letter they were living in a boarding house in Saint-Germain-en-Laye, a suburb of Paris, where they were to stay until their return to Canada in 1950.
20. See note 17.
21. Jean-Marie Nadeau, a Montreal lawyer, was Gabrielle Roy's agent from 1946 to 1960.
22. Keewatin is a village near Kenora where for several years Bernadette was superior of a convent for girls, living "a life of real poverty with a single companion in a shack that barely kept out the rain" (*Enchantment and Sorrow*, p. 102).

23. Excide Landry, the youngest brother of Gabrielle Roy's mother. In the region known as Pembina Mountain, around Somerset, south-west of Winnipeg, this uncle owned a farm on which stood the house that Gabrielle Roy later recalled as "one of the most-loved houses in my life" (*Enchantment and Sorrow*, p. 45). She stayed in this house on many occasions, as a child, a teenager, and in her young adulthood when she was a teacher at Cardinal (see *Enchantment and Sorrow*, p. 32-47, 88-96). Excide's wife Luzina died very young. Gabrielle Roy gave her name to one of the principal characters in *Where Nests the Water Hen.*
24. Saint-Léon is a village near Somerset. This was where Gabrielle Roy's maternal grandparents had settled on their arrival from Quebec; this was also where Gabrielle Roy's parents were married in 1886 and where they lived for a time before moving to Saint-Alphonse, then Mariapolis, then Somerset, and finally Saint-Boniface in 1897. While staying with her uncle, Excide (see note 23), the young Gabrielle used to go to Saint-Léon on occasion to visit "Mémère" Major, Excide's mother-in-law (see *Enchantment and Sorrow*, p. 38-41).
25. Two articles inspired by life in outlying regions of France appeared in subsequent years, "Sainte-Anne-la-Palud" (*Nouvelle revue canadienne*, Ottawa, April-May 1951) and "La Camargue" (*Amérique française*, Montreal, May-June 1952); both were republished in *Fragile Lights of Earth.* As for the pieces "dictated by homesickness", they were most likely stories included in *Where Nests the Water Hen*, Gabrielle Roy's second book, which was begun in 1948 and was published in French in 1950.
26. Major-General Georges Vanier, later Governor General of Canada.
27. This longstanding friend of Gabrielle Roy's had married Henri Bougearel, then French consul in Winnipeg; at the time of this letter he had been assigned to a post in Strasbourg with the newly created Council of Europe.
28. Gabrielle Roy later recalled this visit to Chartres as one of the experiences that helped her to write *Where Nests the Water Hen.* See "Memory and Creation", which was published in French in 1956 and republished in *Fragile Lights of Earth.*
29. See note 21.
30. Anna and Albert Painchaud and their eldest son, Fernand, had houses in Saint-Vital alongside the Red River, which floods frequently in springtime.

31. Gabrielle Roy and her husband returned to Canada late in June 1950. They lived for a time in Ville Lasalle, a suburb of Montreal, before moving permanently to Quebec City in 1951.
32. Bernadette was coming to Quebec City to take a summer course at l'Université Laval.
33. In the early 1950s Clémence had been placed by Bernadette in this home in Winnipeg run by the Sisters of the Presentation, and she had been living there since. She had previously lived at the Foyer Jeanne d'Arc, a home north of Winnipeg, where she had been placed by Aunt Rosalie, sister of Gabrielle Roy's mother.
34. Gabrielle Roy acquired this summer cottage in 1957 and kept it for the rest of her life. Petite-Rivière-Saint-François is on the north shore of the estuary of the Saint Lawrence River, north-east of Quebec City, in the county of Charlevoix, not far from Baie-Saint-Paul.
35. Between *Rue Deschambault* (*Street of Riches*) in 1955 and *La montagne secrète* (*The Hidden Mountain*) in 1961, Gabrielle Roy published no books. In this interval, however, she continued to write stories inspired by her family's history, some of which were published later as *La route d'Altamont* (*The Road Past Altamont*) in 1966 and *De quoi t'ennuies-tu Eveline?* in 1982.
36. Sister Malvina, née Antoinette Kérouack, was and continued to be Bernadette's confidante.
37. The photograph appears on the back cover of this book, and also in François Ricard, *Gabrielle Roy* (Montreal: Fides, 1975), p. 23.
38. Albert Painchaud, Anna's husband.
39. See note 12.
40. Monseigneur Antoine Deschambault of Saint Vital, who blessed Gabrielle Roy's marriage on August 26, 1947, in Saint-Emile Church.
41. Gabrielle Roy's father, Léon Roy, was born in Quebec in 1850 and died in Saint-Boniface on February 20, 1929. See *Enchantment and Sorrow*, p. 26-30, 69-81. He inspired two of the stories in *Street of Riches*, "The Well of Dunrea" and "By Day and by Night".
42. This was Antonine Maillet. Her master's thesis, submitted to l'Université Saint-Joseph in Moncton, New Brunswick, was entitled "La femme et l'enfant dans l'oeuvre de Gabrielle Roy"; her first book, *Pointe-aux-coques*, was published in 1958 (Fides) and republished in 1972 (Leméac).
43. This interview with the journalist Judith Jasmin, produced by Radio-Canada on January 30, 1961, was the only television interview ever granted by Gabrielle Roy.

44. Anna and her husband, Albert, were selling their house at Saint-Vital (see note 4, note 11). Albert Painchaud died a few months later, in October 1961.
45. Germain Roy, brother of Gabrielle and Bernadette, had died the day before in Saint-Boniface from injuries received in a car accident; he was fifty-nine and was survived by his wife, Antonia, and daughters, Lucille and Yolande. He too had made a career of teaching. On Germain and Antonia, see *Enchantment and Sorrow*, p. 147-148.
46. This was a vacation camp for nuns on the shores of Lake Winnipeg, founded by Monseigneur Morton.
47. First to Vienna, where Gabrielle Roy's husband was to attend a medical convention, and then to Greece.
48. Léontine is the wife of Fernand Painchaud, Anna's eldest son, with whom Anna lived for a time after "La Painchaudière" was sold (see note 44).
49. This novel was published first in 1961 by Editions Beauchemin in Montreal and then in Paris in the autumn of 1962 by Flammarion.
50. Yolande Roy, younger daughter of Germain (see note 45), at age twenty was about to marry Jean Cyr of Saint-Vital.
51. Gabrielle and Bernadette's mother was Mélina Landry; she was also called Mina.
52. Except for *The Tin Flute*, which was translated by Hannah Josephson in 1947, it had been Harry L. Binsse who had translated all of Gabrielle Roy's books into English up to this point: *Where Nests the Water Hen*, 1951; *The Cashier*, 1955; *Street of Riches*, 1957. *The Hidden Mountain* was published in 1962 in New York by Harcourt, Brace & World and in Toronto by McClelland & Stewart; it was the last translated by Binsse. Later books were translated by Joyce Marshall, Alan Brown, and, after Gabrielle Roy's death, Patricia Claxton.
53. See note 49.
54. Eliane is the daughter of Uncle Excide Landry (see note 23). She and her husband, Laurent Jubinville, and their six children lived for a time at Camperville on Lake Winnipegosis, where Gabrielle Roy spent the summer of 1936 with them. This experience was one of the sources of inspiration for *Where Nests the Water Hen*. See *Enchantment and Sorrow*, p. 149-151.
55. These were probably stories that later composed *The Road Past Altamont*, 1966.

56. See note 42. *On a mangé la dune,* Antonine Maillet's second novel, was published in 1962 by Editions Beauchemin, Gabrielle Roy's Montreal publisher since 1947.
57. Since the death of her husband a year earlier, Anna, who now possessed assets in the five-figure range, had had no permanent address, living sometimes at Saint-Vital with her son Fernand and his wife Léontine, sometimes with her second son, Paul, in Marmora, Ontario, sometimes in Montreal with her sister Adèle. In November 1962 she was with Gilles, her youngest son, in Cornwall, Pennsylvania, where she was to stay until the end of the year. At this time she was seventy-four years old and in increasingly poor health.
58. This story appeared first in English in *Maclean's Magazine,* December 15, 1962; it appeared in French in *Le Magazine Maclean* in August 1963.
59. With her sister Anna, Bernadette had travelled to Powell River in British Columbia, where their brother Rodolphe (see note 120) was living, employed at the time in a motel.
60. See note 50.
61. Since moving to Quebec City in 1951, Gabrielle Roy and her husband had been living in a small apartment on Grande-Allée. At the time of this letter they had just moved into a larger apartment in the same building, overlooking the Plains of Abraham. This was where Gabrielle Roy lived for the rest of her life.
62. See note 57. After a second stay with her sister Adèle during the winter of 1963, Anna returned to Winnipeg and from there travelled to British Columbia with Bernadette. On their return to Winnipeg she took a room at a hotel, suffering increasingly from cancer of the intestine.
63. The daughter of Eliane and Laurent Jubinville (see note 54) and second cousin to Gabrielle Roy. Monique's sister's name is Céline.
64. After two years on the move (see notes 57 and 62), Anna had left in October 1963 to live in Phoenix, Arizona with her son Fernand and his wife, Léontine.
65. See note 27. At this time, Henri Bougearel was on diplomatic posting in Durban, South Africa; he returned with his family in 1966.

66. See note 64.
67. Anna's second son, Paul Painchaud, his wife, Malvina, and Gilles, Anna's youngest son.
68. Rodolphe Roy, brother of Gabrielle and Bernadette, who was living in British Columbia at this time. See notes 59 and 120.
69. Gabrielle Roy speaks of Anna's death and burial in *Enchantment and Sorrow*, p. 129-131.
70. Fernand and Léontine Painchaud's three adopted children. The family had been living in a trailer park in Phoenix for some time.
71. Anna's will bequeathed money to various institutions and left her sons with modest monthly allowances which they could not transmit to their own heirs. Fernand, the eldest son, received the smallest allowance.
72. Antonia, widow of Germain (see note 45), and her daughter Yolande, wife of Jean Cyr.
73. Somerset, south-west of Winnipeg, was home ground for the Landrys, the family of Gabrielle Roy's mother. See notes 23 and 24.
74. See note 71.
75. Julia Marquis, widow of Joseph (Jos) Roy, brother of Gabrielle and Bernadette; Jos, the eldest of the family, died in November 1956.
76. Pauline Boutal, née Le Goff, was a fashion designer and painter at the time when she and her husband, Arthur Boutal, printer of the newspaper *La Liberté*, were leaders of Le Cercle Molière, an amateur theatre group in which Gabrielle Roy was an actress in the 1930s. See Gabrielle Roy's article entitled "Le Cercle Molière . . . porte ouverte", in *Chapeau bas: réminiscences de la vie théâtrale et musicale du Manitoba français*, Part One (Saint-Boniface: Editions du Blé et Société historique de Saint-Boniface, 1980), p. 115-124.
77. See note 71.
78. Bernadette had obtained permission to visit Gabrielle Roy at Petite-Rivière-Saint-François. She and Clémence spent three weeks there in July 1965.
79. Bernadette had succeeded in placing Clémence in a government-sponsored home at Sainte-Anne-des-Chênes, south-east of Winnipeg. See *Enchantment and Sorrow*, p. 132.
80. Jori Smith and Berthe Simard, friends and neighbours of Gabrielle Roy's at Petite-Rivière-Saint-François.
81. Madeleine Chassé and Madeleine Bergeron of Quebec City, friends of Gabrielle Roy.

82. To Provence, where Gabrielle Roy spent part of the winter. During this trip she also took advantage of the opportunity to see her friend Paula Bougearel (see notes 27 and 65).
83. "Gabrielle Roy, la grande romancière canadienne", an article by Alice Parizeau, with fragments of an interview with Gabrielle Roy, in the French-language magazine *Châtelaine*, April 1966.
84. This book was published first in Montreal by Editions HMH in 1966, then in Paris by Flammarion in 1967. The English translation by Joyce Marshall, *The Road Past Altamont*, was published in New York and Toronto in the autumn of 1966.
85. See note 79.
86. Jean Palmer, a friend of "the Madeleines" (see note 81).
87. At this time there was a plan to film the story "Le vieillard et l'enfant" ("The Old Man and the Child"), one of the four making up *The Road Past Altamont*, but the plan was not carried through. A new film adaptation of this story, by Claude Grenier of the National Film Board, was finally completed in 1986.
88. No doubt the Association d'éducation des Canadiens français, founded in 1916.
89. This text, entitled "Man and His World: The Theme Unfolded by Gabrielle Roy", was published first in 1967 by the Canadian Corporation for the 1967 World Exhibition (Montreal) and was republished in *Fragile Lights of Earth.*
90. See note 89.
91. Yolande, niece of Gabrielle Roy, and her husband, Jean Cyr, were living in Ottawa at this time.
92. See note 33.
93. See note 76.
94. This was the first investiture of the Order of Canada, which came into existence on July 1, 1967; Gabrielle Roy was created a Companion of the Order.
95. Les Etats-Généraux du Canada français (Estates-General of French Canada), organized by the Société Saint-Jean-Baptiste of Montreal, during which independentist sentiment was vigorously expressed.
96. Gabrielle Roy protested publicly against General de Gaulle's "*Vive le Québec libre!*" See *Le Soleil*, July 27, 1967 and *Le Devoir*, July 31, 1967.
97. A Canadian diplomat of Métis origin, whom Gabrielle Roy had known in Manitoba.

98. Bernadette did finally succeed in placing Clémence in Foyer Sainte-Thérèse in Otterburne, a home run by the Sisters of Providence. In *Enchantment and Sorrow* (p. 134-136, 138-142), Gabrielle Roy recounts a visit she made to Clémence here in 1971. Otterburne is south-east of Winnipeg.
99. Sainte-Anne-des-Chênes. See note 79.
100. Léa Lafrenière, née Landry, daughter of Uncle Excide (see note 23), sister of Eliane Jubinville (see note 54).
101. See note 89.
102. Particularly in a letter of November 1955. It would seem that Adèle's animosity began in this period, when she had just published *Le pain de chez nous: histoire d'une famille manitobaine* (Montreal: Editions du Lévrier, 1954) and was resentful when, the following year, Gabrielle published *Street of Riches*, which also drew upon family history. See Adèle's last published work (published under the name Marie-Anna A. Roy), *Le miroir du passé* (Montreal: Québec-Amérique, 1979), p. 206-207.
103. See note 98.
104. Under the name Marie-Anna A. Roy, Adèle had just published, at her own expense, *La Montagne Pembina au temps des colons: historique des paroisses de la région de la Montagne Pembina et biographies des principaux pionniers* (Winnipeg, 1969).
105. Until this time the rules of Bernadette's community had obliged her to sign herself and be addressed by her name in religion, Sister Léon-de-la-Croix, or more simply, Sister Léon. By opening her letters with *Ma chère petite soeur*, Gabrielle Roy had been playing on the double sense of the word *soeur* or "sister" without infringing the rules. See also the letter of April 11, 1970.
106. This was Gabrielle Roy's mother-in-law, who was remarried and living in Saint-Boniface.
107. Adèle, who was fifteen years old when Gabrielle was born, had indeed been chosen to be Gabrielle's godmother; their brother Rodolphe was her godfather.
108. Bernadette had written to Adèle entreating her to withdraw the manuscript in question and destroy it, and on May 12 sent Gabrielle Roy a copy of this letter. Adèle flatly refused to comply and quarrelled with Bernadette.

109. See note 89.
110. A resort area on Lake Winnipeg.
111. Widow of Germain, brother of Gabrielle Roy (see note 45).
112. Widow of Jos, eldest brother of Gabrielle (see note 75).
113. The fourth and last of the stories making up the book by the same name.
114. The village in Saskatchewan where Léon Roy, the father of Gabrielle, settled French-Canadian colonists from Quebec and New England when he was a settlement officer for the federal Department of Immigration (1897-1915). Jos and Julia lived here, as well as Anna and her husband, Albert Painchaud, when they were first married, and also Germain when he became a schoolteacher.
115. Bill 63, introduced by the Union Nationale government, envisaged freedom of choice in language of education, giving rise to a major demonstration on Parliament Hill in Quebec City. This law, the first in a series of language laws, aroused fears that immigrants to Quebec would opt massively for schooling in English, at a time when a drastically reduced birthrate was raising the spectre of the French-speaking population being reduced in a very few years to minority status in the province. See Linteau, P.A., R.Durocher, J.-C. Robert, and F. Ricard, *Histoire du Québec contemporain II: Le Québec depuis 1930* (Montreal: Boréal, second edition, 1989), p. 602-607.
116. See note 54.
117. Blanche is the daughter of Jos, Gabrielle Roy's eldest brother (see note 75).
118. Brother of Gabrielle Roy. See note 120.
119. The corner of the page is missing.
120. Rodolphe Roy, brother of Gabrielle and Bernadette. Unmarried, he was first a stationmaster, then enlisted for service in the Canadian Army during the Second World War. At the time of this letter he had been living for a number of years in Vancouver, where his nephew, Robert Roy (son of Jos), kept a protective eye on him. Bernadette and Anna had already travelled to British Columbia in response to his plea (see note 59). Bernadette did decide to go to him again on this occasion, and was there from late December 1969 to mid-January 1970. Rodolphe died on June 28, 1971. He was Gabrielle Roy's godfather.
121. Eva's precise relationship in the family remains to be established.

122. Bernadette had just been admitted to hospital, where on March 16 she underwent surgery for the removal of a kidney.
123. Widow of Germain Roy (see note 45).
124. Sister Berthe Valcourt, Bernadette's Superior, became Gabrielle Roy's friend and confidante. See *Enchantment and Sorrow*, p. 136-140.
125. This note is undated but must have been written on March 22 or 23. Gabrielle Roy was then in Saint-Boniface, having come from Quebec City to Bernadette's bedside. She stayed for three weeks. On March 22, Gabrielle's birthday, a little party was held in Bernadette's hospital room (see letter of April 12, 1970). Bernadette left the hospital on March 30 and returned to the infirmary of the Académie Saint-Joseph. Gabrielle Roy recalls these weeks spent with the dying Bernadette a number of times in *Enchantment and Sorrow*, p. 126-128, 136, 171-173.
126. Mon enfant, ma soeur,
Songe à la douceur
D'aller là-bas vivre ensemble
Aimer à loisir
Aimer et mourir
Au pays qui te ressemble.
Charles Baudelaire, *L'invitation au voyage*
127. Robert (Bob) Roy and Blanche Roy are children of Jos, the eldest brother of Gabrielle and Bernadette; on Rodolphe Roy, another brother, see note 120; Yolande Cyr, née Roy, is the daughter of Germain, the third and youngest brother of Gabrielle and Bernadette (see note 45).
128. This article appeared in French in *Mosaic*, Winnipeg, Spring 1970, and was republished as "My Manitoba Heritage" in *Fragile Lights of Earth.*
129. Alphonse Allais was a French humorist of the late nineteenth century.
130. Daughters of Gabrielle and Bernadette's uncle Excide Landry. See notes 54 and 100.
131. Regarding this photograph, see the letter of December 6, 1958 and note 37.
132. This may be an allusion to the story "A Bit of Yellow Ribbon" in *Street of Riches*, which recalls Bernadette's entry into religious life. In the story Bernadette is called Odette.
133. Gabrielle Roy was called this in the family during her childhood on account of her delicate health. See the story entitled "Petite Misère" in *Street of Riches.*

134. This book is no doubt *Enchanted Summer*, published two years after *Windflower*. See *Enchantment and Sorrow*, p. 172-173.
135. Sister Berthe Valcourt (see note 124).
136. Gabrielle Roy inadvertently dated this letter April 5, 1970.
137. This film, entitled "Of Many People" ("Un siècle d'hommes"), was a multi-media presentation composed of slides, film footage, and drawings inspired by *Where Nests the Water Hen* and produced by the National Film Board in 1970 for the governments of Canada and Manitoba.
138. The wild geese that congregate on the shores and islands of the Saint Lawrence River below Quebec City are snow geese. Canada geese may appear among them, but not in large numbers.
139. The wife of the painter Jean-Claude Lemieux, who illustrated an art edition of *La Petite Poule d'Eau (Where Nests the Water Hen)* published by Gilles Corbeil in 1971; earlier, in 1953, he also painted a portrait of Gabrielle Roy, which is reproduced in R.-M. Charland and J.-N. Samson, *Gabrielle Roy* (Montreal: Fides, 1972), in the collection "Dossiers de documentation sur la littérature canadienne-française", p.78.
140. Bernadette died on May 25, 1970 at the age of seventy-two.
141. See the letter of December 4, 1969 and note 120.
142. Anna Landry, a sister-in-law of Gabrielle Roy's mother, was living at this time in the vicinity of Somerset, south-west of Winnipeg.

About the Author

Gabrielle Roy was born in St-Boniface, Manitoba, on March 22, 1909. She was a schoolteacher from 1928 to 1937, the year in which she left on an extended trip of two years in France and England on the eve of the Second World War. Returning to Canada in 1939, she decided to settle in Montreal and became a freelance journalist with *Le Jour*, *Le Canada*, *La Revue moderne*, and *Le Bulletin des agriculteurs*, for which she wrote stories and several major series of articles. Her first novel, *Bonheur d'occasion*, was awarded the Prix Femina in France in 1947, and its translation, *The Tin Flute*, was chosen as the Book of the Month by the Literary Guild of America. While in Europe once again from 1947 to 1950 with her husband, Dr. Marcel Carbotte, she wrote her second book, *La Petite Poule d'Eau (Where Nests the Water Hen)*. She returned to live in Quebec, where she remained and wrote for the rest of her life. She died in Quebec City on July 13, 1983.

Gabrielle Roy wrote sixteen books besides this collection of letters, comprising novels, short stories, children's books, an autobiography, and a collection of essays. She also wrote a number of other essays and articles. Her recognition as one of the leading figures in Canadian and Quebec literature is attested by the many honours she received, including three Governor General's Awards (1947, 1957, and 1978), the Prix Femina (France, 1947), the Lorne Pierce Medal (Royal Society of Canada, 1947), the Medal of the Académie canadienne-française (1947), the Prix Duvernay (1956), the Prix David (1971), and the Canada Council Prize for Children's Literature (1979).

About the Translator

Patricia Claxton is a member of the Society of Translators of Quebec and the Literary Translators' Association, of which she was founding president, and for eight years was a teacher of translation. She has translated books by Gabrielle Roy, Nicole Brossard, Cécile Gagnon, Fernand Ouellet, and Marcel Trudel, and stories, poems, and articles by Naïm Kattan, Andrée Maillet, André Major, André Roy, France Théoret, and Pierrè Elliott Trudeau. She won the Governor General's Award for her translation of *Enchantment and Sorrow,* Gabrielle Roy's autobiography, and has won three Canada Council Honorable Mentions for other translations.

The Works of Gabrielle Roy

Second and subsequent Canadian editions listed are revised editions, excepting special editions as noted.

Bonheur d'occasion, Montreal, 1945, 1947, 1965, 1970, 1977; Paris, 1947, Geneva, 1968. Prix Femina; Book of the Month, Literary Guild of America; Medal of the Académie canadienne-française; Governor General's Award; Lorne Pierce Medal, Royal Society of Canada. English translation by Hannah Josephson, *The Tin Flute,* Toronto, McClelland & Stewart, 1947. Retranslation by Alan Brown, Toronto, McClelland & Stewart, 1980. Spanish, Danish, Swedish, Norwegian, Slovak, Czech, Romanian, and Russian translations.

La Petite Poule d'Eau, Montreal, 1950, 1957, 1970, 1980; Paris, 1951, 1967; Geneva, 1953; numbered art edition with twenty prints by Jean-Paul Lemieux, Montreal, 1971. English translation by Harry Binsse, *Where Nests the Water Hen,* Toronto, McClelland & Stewart, 1951. German translation.

Alexandre Chenevert, Montreal, 1954, 1973, 1979; Paris, 1954. English translation by Harry Binsse, *The Cashier,* Toronto, McClelland & Stewart, 1955. German translation.

Rue Deschambault, Montreal, 1955, 1956, 1967, 1971, 1980. Governor General's Award. English translation by Harry Binsse, *Street of Riches,* Toronto, McClelland & Stewart, 1957. Italian translation.

La Montagne secrète, Montreal, 1961, 1971, 1974, 1978; Paris, 1962; numbered deluxe edition illustrated by René Richard, Montreal, 1975. English translation by Harry Binsse, *The Hidden Mountain,* Toronto, McClelland & Stewart, 1962.

La Route d'Altamont, Montreal, 1966, 1979; Paris, 1967. English translation by Joyce Marshall, *The Road Past Altamont,* Toronto, McClelland & Stewart, 1966. German translation.

La Rivière sans repos, novel preceded by three short stories, Montreal, 1970, 1971, 1979; Paris, 1972. English translation (novel only) by Joyce Marshall, *Windflower,* Toronto, McClelland & Stewart, 1970. English translation by Joyce Marshall of the three short stories is pending.

Cet été qui chantait, Quebec and Montreal, 1972, 1973; Montreal, 1979. English translation by Joyce Marshall, *Enchanted Summer,* Toronto, McClelland & Stewart, 1976.

Un Jardin au bout du monde, Montreal, 1975, 1981. English translation by Alan Brown, *Garden in the Wind,* Toronto, McClelland & Stewart, 1977.

Ma Vache Bossie (children's story), Montreal, 1976, 1982. English translation by Alan Brown, *My Cow Bossie,* Toronto, McClelland & Stewart, 1988. English and French editions illustrated by Louise Pominville.

Ces enfants de ma vie, Montreal, 1977, 1983. Governor General's Award. English translation by Alan Brown, *Children of My Heart,* Toronto, McClelland & Stewart, 1979.

Fragiles lumières de la terre, Montreal, 1978, 1980, 1982. English translation by Alan Brown, *The Fragile Lights of Earth,* Toronto, McClelland & Stewart, 1982.

Courte-Queue (children's story), Montreal, 1979, 1980. Canada Council Prize for Children's Literature. English translation by Alan Brown, *Cliptail,* Toronto, McClelland & Stewart, 1980. English and French editions illustrated by François Olivier.

De quoi t'ennuies-tu Eveline? suivi de *Ely! Ely! Ely!,* Montreal, 1979, 1982, 1984. English translation by Patricia Claxton pending.

La Détresse et l'enchantement (autobiography), Montreal, 1984. English translation by Patricia Claxton, *Enchantment and Sorrow,* Toronto, Lester & Orpen Dennys, 1987. Governor General's Award for Translation.

La Pékinoise et l'Espagnole (children's story), Montreal, 1987. English translation by Patricia Claxton, *The Tortoiseshell and the Pekinese*, Toronto, Doubleday Canada, 1989. English and French editions illustrated by Jean-Yves Ahern.